Promoting Emotional Education

The 'Innovative Learning for All' series
Series editor: Professor Paul Cooper

The 'Innovative Learning for All' series features accessible books that reveal how schools and educators can meet the needs of vulnerable students, encouraging them to engage in learning and to feel confident in the classroom. Grounded in the latest innovative practice and research, these books offer positive guidance on improving the educational standards for all children by ensuring the most vulnerable are supported.

also in the series

Promoting Resilience in the Classroom
A Guide to Developing Pupils' Emotional and Cognitive Skills
Carmel Cefai
ISBN 978 1 84310 565 7

Nurture Groups in School and at Home
Connecting with Children with Social, Emotional and Behavioural Difficulties
Paul Cooper and Yonca Tiknaz
ISBN 978 1 84310 528 2

of related interest

Educating Difficult Adolescents
Effective Education for Children in Public Care or with Emotional and Behavioural Difficulties
David Berridge, Cherilyn Dance, Jennifer Beecham and Sarah Field
ISBN 978 1 84310 681 4
Quality Matters in Children's Services

Helping Children with Complex Needs Bounce Back
Resilient Therapy[(TM)] for Parents and Professionals
Kim Aumann and Angie Hart
Illustrated by Chloe Gerhardt
ISBN 978 1 84310 948 8

Quick, Easy and Effective Behaviour Management Ideas for the Classroom
Nicola S. Morgan
ISBN 978 1 84310 951 8

Social Skills Games for Children
Deborah M. Plummer
Illustrated by Jane Serrurier
Foreword by Professor Jannet Wright
ISBN 978 1 84310 617 3

Helping Children to Build Self-Esteem
A Photocopiable Activities Book
2nd edition
Deborah M. Plummer
Illustrated by Alice Harper
ISBN 978 1 84310 488 9

Promoting Emotional Education

Engaging Children and Young People with
Social, Emotional and Behavioural Difficulties

**Edited by
Carmel Cefai
and Paul Cooper**

Foreword by
Paul Cooper

Jessica Kingsley Publishers
London and Philadelphia

First published in 2009
by Jessica Kingsley Publishers
116 Pentonville Road
London N1 9JB, UK
and
400 Market Street, Suite 400
Philadelphia, PA 19106, USA

www.jkp.com

Library of Congress Cataloging in Publication Data
Promoting emotional education : engaging children and young people with social, emotional and behavioural difficulties / edited by Carmel Cefai and Paul Cooper.
     p. cm.
   Includes bibliographical references and index.
   ISBN 978-1-84310-996-9 (pb : alk. paper) 1. Emotional Intelligence. 2. Emotions and cognition. 3. Emotions in children. 4. Emotions in adolescence. 5. Learning, Psychology of I. Cefai, Carmel. II. Cooper, Paul, 1955-
   BF576.P76 2009
   152.4--dc22

                              2009009518

British Library Cataloguing in Publication Data
A CIP catalogue record for this book is available from the British Library

ISBN 978 1 84310 996 9

Printed and bound in Great Britain by
MGP Books Group, Cornwall

Contents

Introduction

Part 1: Listening to Students' Voices

Part 2: Mobilising Peer Support

Part 3: Working with Students' Emotions

Conclusion

List of Figures

List of Tables

Series Editor's Foreword

The twin needs to raise educational standards for all and to improve access to educational opportunities for the most vulnerable members of society, continue to be major challenges facing educators throughout the world. The persistent link between socio-economic status and educational attainment is one of the few truly dependable outcomes of social scientific research. Children who come from socially deprived backgrounds are at much greater risk of educational failure than children who come from more privileged backgrounds. In the USA, for example, in 1979 individuals from the top income quartile were four times more likely to successfully complete a four-year college degree programme than individuals from the bottom quartile (Barton 1997). By 1994 the disparity had increased from 4 to 10 times (*ibid*). In the UK similar concerns have been noted by the DfES (2004). There is a further association between educational failure and social, emotional and behavioural difficulties (*ibid*), as well as an association between social, emotional and behavioural problems and social disadvantage (Schneiders, Drukker, Ende *et al.* 2003).

The interaction between socio-economic, educational and socio-emotional factors is clearly complex and multi-faceted. It is certainly not the case that any one of these factors necessarily precedes either of the others. Resilience factors of various kinds come into play for some people, enabling them, as individuals, to buck the statistical trends. Temperament, social and cognitive strategies, personal values, external social support structures, and parental personality characteristics, can help to create opportunities for unpredicted positive educational and socio-emotional outcomes for individuals who appear to be in the most dire socio-economic circumstances (Rutter 1987). Unfortunately, there are counterbalancing risk factors, which will combine with disadvantage for other people to create serious life problems (e.g. Patterson, Reid and Dishion 1992).

It is all too easy to place the blame for a child's educational failure and disruptive behaviour on family and/or neighbourhood factors, and to write-off whole geographical areas as being populated by 'undesirables'. It is perhaps because of the dangers of provocative, negative stereotyping of this kind that we sometimes neglect the socio-economic correlates of educational disengagement and social, emotional and behavioural difficulties.

A crucial factor that can be both a cause and effect of educational failure is what David Smith, in the Edinburgh Study of Youth Transitions and Crime, describes as 'attachment to school' (Smith 2006). Attachment to school can be defined in terms of the degree of commitment towards and engagement with schooling that students feel. Students who have a strong attachment to school have feelings of attachment to teachers, and believe that success in school will lead to significant rewards in later life. Weak attachment to school is characterised by indifference or hostility towards teachers and scepticism about the value of schooling. Weak attachment to school can lead to disaffection and alienation. These are problems of a psychological nature that impair the individual's capacity for social and academic engagement that can, in turn, lead to reduced life chances.

Innovative Learning for All offers a series of publications each of which considers ways in which schools in the 21st century can address the needs of vulnerable students and contribute to their effective attachment to school and engagement with educational opportunities. Each author in the series offers insights into different ways in which these goals can be achieved by drawing on the best available, and in some cases original, research evidence. At the heart of the series is the shared view that educational standards for everyone will improve if we focus our efforts on promoting the educational engagement of the most vulnerable. There is also a strong consensus around the need to value all children and young people as individuals and to maintain a commitment to their positive growth, and for these values to be translated into practical support that is informed by a firm conceptual and technical understanding.

This is not to say that education is a cure all for the dysfunctions of society. Far from it, the ideas and practices described in this series depend upon political will and government action to achieve their best. On the other hand, the programmes and approaches dealt with in this series will not be made redundant by enlightened and effective measures that address social and economic deprivation. However, they will, undoubtedly, be aided by such measures. It follows, therefore, that the authors in this series all hope that some of the ideas that they put forward will contribute to both the thinking and practice of educators as well as politicians.

Paul Cooper, University of Leicester

REFERENCES

Barton, Paul E. (1997) *Towards Inequality: Disturbing Trends in Higher Education.* Available online at www.ets.org/portal/site/ets, accessed 22 May 2009.

DfES (2004) *Breaking the Cycle.* London: DfES.

Patterson, G., Reid, J. and Dishion, T. (1992) *Anti-Social Boys,* vol. 4. Eugene, OR: Castalia.

Rutter, M. (1987) 'Psychosocial resilience and protective mechanisms.' *American Journal of Orthopsychiatry 57*, 3.

Schneiders, J., Drukker, M., van der Ende, J., Verhulst, J., van Os, J. and Nicolson, N. (2003) 'Neighbourhood socio-economic disadvantage and behavioural problems from late childhood into early adolescence.' *Journal of Epidemiology and Community Health 57*, 699–703.

Smith, D. (2006) School Experience and Delinquency at Ages 13 to 16. Edinburgh: Centre for Law and Society, University of Edinburgh.

Introduction

CHAPTER 1

Emotional Education: Connecting with Students' Thoughts and Emotions

Carmel Cefai and Paul Cooper

A century ago, John Dewey was already underlining the social and emotional nature of the classroom and the relationship between social processes and learning. There is a history of educational approaches influenced by these ways of thinking, such as those developed by Maria Montessori, A.S. Neill, D. Wills and Bruno Bettelheim. Yet for the most part, mainstream education in the 20th century has been characterised by practices focusing on the acquisition of knowledge, with little attention to social and emotional learning. The third 'force' in education has found it difficult to make any deep inroads into the mainstream curriculum and gain the value accredited to literacy and numeracy. Although educators are usually aware of the importance of the socio-emotional dimension in education, they have been facing consistent pressure to ensure ever higher levels of student performance and passes in examinations. As a result, many schools and teachers have been constrained, against their better judgement, to reduce the amount of attention they pay to students' social and emotional needs and to classroom relationships. The recent focus on league tables and performance indicators has continued to separate the cognitive from the affective dimensions of education, promoting and pushing the former at the expense of the latter. As Chris Watkins succinctly put it:

> politicians and policy makers have reduced the goal of schools and colleges to measurable outcomes of a limited sort: performance tables, performance pay and performance management. From the confines of their parallel universe, they create and disperse lists by which all shall be

judged…under such pressures there is a grave risk that teachers pass this on to pupils. (Watkins 2003, p.8)

The past couple of decades however, have seen the rise of emotions in education, with a growing movement for a more humanistic, holistic and socio-emotional approach to educational practices. Schools and classrooms are being called to go beyond measurable standards and performance indicators and become more engaged with the real world and help in the formation of academically, socially and emotionally literate young people (e.g. Battistich 2001; Cefai 2008; Elias, Arnold and Steiger Hussey 2003). The notions of emotional intelligence and emotional literacy have become current buzzwords in education, underlying the role of emotions in learning and behaviour. Recent research in neuroscience has made us revisit some of our previously held beliefs about learning and child development, underlining the inextricable links between cognitive and emotional development and the key role of emotions in learning. In evolutionary terms the development of the faculties of emotion (the seat of emotions is in the most primitive area of the brain, the amygdala), precedes that of the higher social and cognitive functions. The dominance of the amygdala on the cortex underlines the critical influence of emotions on cognition. For instance fear and anxiety cause the blood flow to move away from the neocortex, the seat of cognitive processes, towards the brain stem, while a relaxed and positive affect state triggers neurochemical changes conducive to learning (Geake 2006; Geake and Cooper 2003). Clearly, the integration of thoughts and emotions in education would facilitate and optimise the learning process.

The recent shift towards a broader educational agenda has also been brought about by the realisation that the exclusive focus on academic learning was not only creating stress and anxiety at a vulnerable age in the lives of children and young persons, but students were leaving school without the necessary competencies and resources to face the 'tests of life' (Elias 2001). Questions have been raised about the value and effectiveness of an educational system that had become out of tune with the realities and challenges of the 21st century. Young people were leaving school without the adequate competencies necessary to function as successful and resilient citizens. As Nel Noddings (1992) put it: 'the traditional organization of schooling is intellectually and morally inadequate for contemporary society. We live in an age troubled by social problems that force us to reconsider what we do in schools' (p.173).

As they seek to establish themselves as autonomous and resilient citizens in a fast-changing world, young people will need to have the competencies and resources to achieve their goals, to solve problems effectively, to engage in healthy relationships and to sustain their psychological and social wellbeing. When they leave school, students will need to have learned the requisite academic and scientific skills to enable them to function as self-reliant citizens and to gain access to opportunities and resources. They also need, however, to be equipped with the skills to be flexible in the face of change, to be creative in problem-solving and effective in decision-making, to build and maintain supportive relationships, to work collaboratively with others, to mobilise their resources in times of difficulty. Seen in this way, an educational system with an exclusive focus on academic performance would thus be shortchanging today's children and young people, and denying them their basic right for a holistic and relevant education as a preparation for the world outside school.

Academic and socio-emotional literacy are not mutually exclusive or developed at the expense of one another. Indeed they can support, reinforce and complement each other. Happy and socially competent individuals are in the end more productive in schools and society (Layard 2005). Moreover, this educational approach does not only benefit the individual himself or herself, but society as a whole; skills such as empathy, solidarity, tolerance, collaboration, constructive conflict resolution, and emotional regulation, will help to create more harmonious and supportive communities (Noddings 2003).

Effective social and cognitive functioning in children and young people is predicated on emotional competence, which involves the understanding and regulation of emotions as well as the ability to read and empathise with the emotional state of others (cf. Bowlby 1975; Maslow 1970). Psychodynamic theory convincingly argues that the emotional functions need to be regulated by the cognitive, and this is reflected in the modern notions of emotional intelligence and emotional literacy. In the absence of emotional competence, individuals are prone to instinctual responses to basic emotional drives, particularly fear, which in turn lead to an overemphasis of basic fight-or-flight responses. Various terms have been used interchangeably to define this process, such as emotional intelligence (Goleman 1996), emotional literacy (Weare 2003) and social and emotional learning (Elias 2001). We prefer the term *emotional education*, which may be defined as the process by which an individual develops emotional competence, which in turn develops through a social learning process. Emotional education is concerned with the broad, multifactorial nature of learning, which includes the biological, emotional, cognitive and social aspects of learning. This suggests a comprehensive, holistic and biopsychosocial model of education. In this respect, 'emotional education' is broader and more inclusive than other terms used in this area, such as 'emotional intelligence', 'emotional literacy', 'social and emotional learning' and 'social competence'. For instance, emotional intelligence is primarily focused on the cognitive aspect of emotions, while the views of emotional education on learning are broader than those of emotional literacy. Emotional education involves both learning and the promotion of learning, hence incorporating and going beyond social and emotional learning. It is also the process by which socio-emotional competence develops. While the term 'emotional development' involves the automatic development of emotions that may be both functional and dysfunctional, emotional education involves a proactive approach to the promotion of functional and healthy emotional development.

Emotional education diverges in significant ways from practices associated with traditional approaches to 'mainstream' education, which have tended to emphasise teaching and learning as transmission, students as subordinate to teachers' authority, and student docility and passivity as functional traits. By contrast, an emotionally literate approach to education recognises that non-compliant behaviour and disaffection among students is caused or (at least and probably more often) exacerbated by these 'traditional' approaches. The remedy is to employ educational practices that encourage feelings of emotional security in students, and the development of high self-esteem based on trusting and supportive educational relationships. This, in turn, leads to student confidence and autonomy, which are essential qualities for healthy personal development. These qualities are also necessary attributes for economic viability in the 21st century (cf. Layard 2005). This overarching theme is reflected in two major areas in this book: first, the significance of involving and including students in issues related to their and their peers' learning and behaviour; and second, the key role of emotions in students' social and academic behaviour. These two themes are interlinked and intertwined throughout.

The contributions to this volume address these themes in various ways, drawing on empirical evidence for support. Part 1 consists of various chapters presenting students' own concerns and feelings about aspects of their educational experiences, and underlines how listening to students' voices is vital to their positive emotional development. Opportunities for students to express their thoughts and feelings, and for these to be actively listened to by teachers, are vital for positive development. This also underlines the need for students to be equipped with the necessary skills to articulate clearly their feelings and thoughts. In Chapter 2, Frances Toynbee describes how researching the perspectives of students with social, emotional and behaviour difficulties (SEBD) can illuminate the debate about what aspects of provision are considered to be most helpful by the students themselves. In the highly contested arena of 'inclusion' and 'segregation', it is argued that students themselves can enrich the discourse by describing their experiences of policy as played out in individual narratives. The chapter discusses the student perspective literature, with particular reference to the epistemological, ethical and practical reasons for seeking the perspectives of pupils with SEBD. The position taken by the author is that children have equal value to adults, thus their views on the effectiveness of provision provide an essential strand in evidence-based assessment of the value of the interventions made.

Next, our chapter on the narratives of pupils with SEBD on their school experiences, shares similar strands with the former one, arguing how lack of student 'inclusion' and participation in decisions related to educational interventions and provisions, may lead to disengagement on the part of the students. The chapter presents five main themes identified in a review of studies on the views of disengaged and disaffected students in Maltese schools, namely poor relationships with teachers, victimisation by teachers and peers, oppression and powerlessness, unconnected learning experiences, and exclusion and stigmatisation. The nature of the themes underline the universality of students' feelings and concerns, and of their desire to be listened to, respected and valued as human beings.

In another study carried out with former students in Malta, Damian Spiteri presents in Chapter 4 the findings of a study that evaluated the educational interventions at a school for students with SEBD in Malta. The study is based on the participants' own accounts of their lived educational experiences, experience they then used as 'strengths' in their adult lives. The study seeks to illuminate how such processes as their attending this particular school, the peer interactions that they fostered there, and their interactions with the staff and other professionals, served to influence their decisions, both when at school and when eventually they started their own lives as young adults. Rather than focusing on this period as an isolated aspect or period of their lives, the author adopts a life-course approach that is geared to exploring 'the total space' (Levy 1991) in which the lives of these young persons evolved.

The students' views on personal and social education as a separate school subject in Maltese schools and its relevance to their social and emotional development, are presented in Chapter 5. Mark Borg and Andrew Triganza Scott found that personal and social development is overwhelmingly popular among primary and secondary students. Primary school students described it as an interesting, 'fun' subject that allowed discussion, thinking and the sharing of ideas, and that helped them understand others. Similarly, secondary students gave 'interesting topics' and 'preparation for life', as the main reason.

'Assertiveness' and 'decision-making' were indicated by each of the two age groups of students as the two most popular topics. Students found this subject highly relevant to their personal and socio-emotional development, and expressed the wish that more time would be devoted to this area of the curriculum.

The second part of the book develops the issue of student empowerment by exploring how peer-mediated approaches help to enhance the social and academic engagement of students. Positive social and cognitive development is contingent on a healthy emotional climate, which is strongly influenced by the peer group. Peer support is a widely used anti-bullying intervention in both primary and secondary schools, and involves training young people to work together to support victimised peers and to promote alternative, non-violent ways of responding to conflict. In the first chapter in this section, Helen Cowie reviews the major influences on the development of peer support as a bullying prevention intervention in schools. While the benefit for those providing support is clearly document, there is less consistent evidence on the impact of peer support systems on the general climate of the school. The author presents new research and practice findings that may help us to understand how and why change can be effected in this area. The conclusions relate to the wider context of the developing role of peer support in schools today in terms of minimising violent and bullying behaviour.

The next two chapters present the findings of two studies in Quebec, Canada, on peer tutoring and students with social, emotional and behaviour difficulties. In Chapter 7, Anastasia Karagiannakis and Ingrid Sladeczek discuss the effectiveness of one particular form of peer support, *classwide peer tutoring*, on the academic and socio-emotional behaviour of young Canadian school-aged boys with SEBD. They present the findings of a study that investigated the boys' academic performance, on-task behaviour, self-concept and school satisfaction, following the implementation of a peer-support programme. They found positive academic and socio-emotional effects amongst the students receiving peer tutoring, and suggest how the system may be employed to promote a more inclusive system for students with SEBD. In Chapter 8, Claire Beaumont shows how students with SEBD can benefit from being peer helpers themselves. After training such students to act as mediators or peer counsellors, Claire and her colleagues observed an improvement in their self-control, expression, and self-esteem, and a decrease in aggressive behaviour. An analysis of the conversations held with these helpers revealed various benefits connected with the experience of peer support, such as social acceptance, a sense of belonging, identifying and empathising with the feelings of others, and academic motivation. These positive effects support the hypothesis that we can positively influence the social skills of young persons with SEBD by putting them in touch with the feelings of others and by allowing them to help their peers.

Circle Time is a child-friendly approach encouraging the practice of socio-emotional skills in an inclusive, caring and democratic climate, with the peer group itself acting as an empowering vehicle for the promotion of emotional education. It provides a very good platform for the practice of skills such as speaking, listening, turn-taking, problem-solving, understanding one's emotion and enjoying and appreciating each other's company. Jenny Mosley's approach to raising self-esteem, promoting positive behaviour, encouraging supported self-discipline, and creating co-operative learning environments, has been encapsulated in the Quality Circle Time model. In Chapter 9, Mosley provides the reader the opportunity to explore in more depth this approach as a tool to develop the social and emotional competencies in children and young persons. The chapter reviews the existing evidence for the effectiveness of Quality Circle Time in the promotion of socio-emotional competence, and describes the practical steps in organising Quality Circle Time in the classroom.

The third part of the book presents various studies on emotion-based approaches in education, such as nurture groups and anger management, and explains how these interventions are related to healthy positive social and academic outcomes. In the first chapter, Paul Cooper introduces nurture groups as a therapeutic educational approach for young children with social, emotional and behaviour difficulties. The chapter describes the development of this approach in the UK and evaluates its effectiveness in terms of academic and social and emotional outcomes. In his review of research, Cooper draws on a lengthy programme of research, including a major national study carried out by the author himself, as well as a wide range of other studies carried out by practitioners and researchers. The author shows that there are certain consistently replicated findings that point to the value of nurture groups as an effective form of educational provision. He also considers evidence of some of the challenges that nurture groups face in their development. Marion Bennathan, one of the pioneers in the establishment of nurture groups in the UK, focuses in Chapter 11 on the relationship between early socio-emotional experiences and mental health in adulthood, drawing on recent developments in neuroscience and pharmacology to illustrate this relationship. She describes how nurture groups have been developed to provide for healthy early relationships amongst children who may be at risk, and underlines the usefulness of such groups as an effective tool in the emotional education of young children with SEBD.

Kangaroo Groups are an adaption of nurture groups in Quebec, Canada, consisting of small groups of students with behaviour difficulties attending mainstream primary schools. In this next chapter, Caroline Couture describes the adaptations made to the original nurture group model to fit the culture and reality of Quebec's schools, and then presents the findings of a study that evaluated the effectiveness of this provision in its first year of implementation. The study investigated the impact of the intervention on the students' attention, behaviour and emotional development. Couture concludes that overall, the results placed Kangaroo Groups amongst the promising educational provisions for students with SEBD.

The final chapter in this section examines a different emotion-based intervention, namely agression replacement training (ART), and its application in Norwegian schools. ART has been originally developed by Arnold Goldstein and his colleagues in the USA (Goldstein, Glick and Gibbs 1998) as a tool to help people with anger-control difficulties to learn new prosocial behaviors to replace behaviours such as verbal or physical aggression and withdrawal. In this chapter Knut Gundersen and Froe Svartdal, who have been undertaking research, practice and training in ART in Norway for the past decade, discuss the effectiveness of ART with children and young people with behaviour difficulties in Norway. They found improved social and emotional competence amongst the programme participants, and the programme appears to provide a promising approach to emotional regulation both amongst students with SEBD and those without such difficulties.

In the concluding chapter, we draw together some of the key themes developed in the book and place them within the context of an analysis of the cultural values surrounding parenting, childhood, children and young people. The chapter concludes with a call for a more positive approach to understanding and defining childhood and adolescence as important life stages that make a vital contribution to society. We underline the misleading nature of what may pass for adult self-actualisation through sheer materialism and selfishness, with children and parenting seen as obstacles to the adults' path to fulfilment and self-actualisation. It is argued that children may well be one of the most direct pathways to adult self-actualisation. If as adults we wish to be genuine self-actualisers, then we need to work towards the creation of a world in which children develop as well-balanced, emotionally secure and socially engaged citizens. This requires the adult world to become more constructively engaged with children and their needs. The more adults open up the channels of communication with children and young people, and listen to their opinions, the more opportunity there will be for dialogue and sharing of perspectives, and consequently for a better world for both adults and children.

This book examines the various facets of emotional education, in various ways, and across a range of contexts, cultures and countries. It does not claim to provide an exhaustive, inclusive or comprehensive account of emotional education. We see this publication as an attempt to contribute to the discussion of this critical aspect of development and education of children and young persons, bringing together a number of international authors, researchers and practitioners who have been working in this area. The chapters provide snapshots of emotional education from differing angles, and contribute to the area in a variety of aspects, particularly the role of emotions in education, and student voice and empowerment. The book should be useful to researchers and practitioners interested in developing approaches to the promotion of emotional education amongst children and young people. Academic researchers, initial and in-service teacher educators, practitioners working with children and young people with SEBD, including school staff and professionals such as psychologists, counsellors and social workers, and directors of services and policy makers, will all find this publication beneficial in their work. It is also our hope that this book will serve to generate further studies and publications in this area.

REFERENCES

Battistich, V. (2001) 'Effects of an Elementary School Intervention on Students' "Connectedness" to School and Social Adjustment During Middle School.' *Resilience in Education: Theoretical, Interactive and Empirical Applications*. Symposium conducted at the annual meeting of the American Educational Research Association. Seattle, WA.

Bowlby, J. (1975) *Attachment and Loss*. London: Penguin.

Cefai, C. (2008) *Promoting Resilience in the Classroom: A Guide to Developing Pupils' Emotional and Cognitive Skills*. London: Jessica Kingsley Publishers.

Elias, M.J. (2001) 'Prepare children for the tests of life, not a life of tests.' *Education Week 21*, 4, 40.

Elias, M.J., Arnold, H. and Steiger Hussey, C. (2003) 'EQ, IQ, and Effective Learning and Leadership.' In M.J. Elias, H. Arnold and C. Steiger Hussey (eds) *EQ+IQ=Best Leadership Practices for Caring and Successful Schools*. Thousands Oaks, CA: Corwin Press.

Geake, J.G. (2006) 'The neurological basis of intelligence: A contrast with "brain-based" education.' *Education-Line*. Available at www.leeds.ac.uk/educol/documents/156074.htm (retrieved 1 March 2009).

Geake, J.G. and Cooper, P.W. (2003) 'Implications of cognitive neuroscience for education.' *Westminster Studies in Education 26*, 10, 7–20.

Goldstein, A.P., Glick, B. and Gibbs, J.C. (1998) *Aggression Replacement Training: A Comprehensive Intervention for Aggressive Youth* (Rev. edition). Champaign, IL: Research Press.

Goleman, D. (1996) *Emotional Intelligence*. London: Bloomsbury.

Layard, R. (2005) *Happiness: Lessons from a New Science*. London: Penguin.

Levy, R. (1991) 'Status Passages as Critical Life-course Transitions.' In W.R. Heinz (ed.) *Theoretical Advances in Life-course Research*. Weinheim: Deutscher Studien Verlag.

Maslow, A. (1970) *Motivation and Personality*. New York: Harper & Row.
Noddings, N. (1992) *The Challenge of Care in Schools*. New York: Teachers College Press.
Noddings, N. (2003) *Happiness and Education*. Cambridge: Cambridge University Press.
Weare, C. (2003) *Developing the Emotionally Literate School*. London: Paul Chapman Educational Publishing.
Watkins, C. (2003) *Learning: A Sense-maker Guide*. London: Association of Teachers and Lecturers.

PART 1

Listening to Students' Voices

CHAPTER 2

The Perspectives of Young People with SEBD about Educational Provision

Frances Toynbee

INTRODUCTION

This chapter discusses how researching the perspectives of pupils with social, emotional and behavioural difficulties (SEBD) can illuminate the debate about what aspects of provision are considered to be most helpful by the pupils themselves. It will be argued that pupils themselves can enrich the discourse by describing their experiences of policy as played out in individual narratives. The ethical and practical reasons for seeking the perspectives of pupils with SEBD will be discussed. The position taken by this author is that children have equal value to adults, and thus, their views on the effectiveness of provision provides an essential strand in evidence based assessment of the value of the interventions made. There are practical and ontological reasons for exploring pupils' perceptions: what adults infer and assume about the educational experience of pupils needs to be examined. Toynbee (1999) found that while pupils in specialist provision reported on positive experiences with their learning and relationships, a majority would prefer to have accessed mainstream schools successfully. The epistemological position taken in the chapter will therefore be that children with SEBD have essential evidence to share about their educational experiences.

WHY ARE PUPIL PERSPECTIVES IMPORTANT?
An epistemological position

To acknowledge that what children and young people think is a valid research focus requires a particular epistemological perspective. This perspective sees people as actively constructing their own meanings: 'We should…assume that children actively engage in construing themselves and learning about the world through social interactions which themselves shape the structure and pattern of their cognition' (Wearmouth 1999, p.17).

Accepting that children as agents are actively making meaning and sense of their surroundings then leads to the necessity for researchers/educators to understand what meanings are being made. For children with SEBD, this is particularly significant, as these are children who are creating particular difficulties for schools (Ofsted 2004). Wearmouth (1999) argues that this constructivist perspective is valuable as it enables us to develop some understanding of how children with SEBD construct their behaviour and in particular, what purpose their behaviour serves.

Pupils in schools can provide a richly layered account of their experiences which reveals how they can and do 'resist attempts to label or exclude them and to seek alternative identities and experiences' (Allan 1999, p.3). Allan (*ibid.*) argues that the dominant discourse, which treats pupils with special needs as passive subjects upon whom 'expert' knowledge is exercised, silences the voice of the pupils. An example of this is the abstract of an article (Hamill and Boyd 2002) that describes pupils 'perceived as disruptive, disaffected and troubled' as 'surprisingly articulate' (p.111). However, pupil voice needs to be seen as an essential part of the 'complex power/knowledge knot' (Allan 1999, p.1), which she argues moves the special needs discourse beyond reductive concerns with placement and practice. The production of 'knowledge' then can be seen as a more dynamic interaction between professional discourses and the perception of pupils, with the acceptance that there is not one simple 'truth' to be revealed, but a series of competing and conflicting narratives that can illuminate the complexity of the processes enacted in schools.

Cooper (2003) argues that 'first hand testimony from the students themselves is an invaluable source of data when trying to assess the values of a school that are reflected in its actual practices, rather than in its policies alone' (p.5). Seeking this 'testimony' can enable practitioners and policy makers to develop a richer and more multi-layered understanding of the ways in which schools function and are experienced by pupils as well as staff. The distinction that Cooper (2003) makes between stated policy and practice can be teased out and examined fully only when pupils are asked how they experience their education. In their study in mainstream schools, Clark *et al.* (1999) found what they considered to be fundamentally exclusionary practices being played out in schools with avowedly 'inclusive' policies. However, the schools did not consider how the pupils experienced these practices, and whether they too considered themselves to be marginalised by these practices. It could be argued that without exploring pupil perspectives, descriptions of schools will always be limited and reductive, as they will only represent the views of adults judging, researching or working within them.

Epistemologically, the position taken by this author is that the voice of pupils with SEBD provides an essential element in the discussion about policy and practice. However, pupils can give us more than evidence about practice. They can enrich our understanding of the processes and power relations that we think we understand, but that in reality, is limited by our partial adult/professional perspective.

An ethical position

The ethical dimension to making children's perspectives a focus of enquiry requires an acceptance that children have a right to be listened to and heard. The right of children to be listened to is enshrined in Article 12 of the United Nations Convention on the Rights of the Child (1989). Lloyd-Smith and Tarr (2000) offer ethical, practical and epistemological reasons for researching children's perspectives using a sociological perspective:

> The reality experienced by children and young people in educational settings cannot be fully comprehended by inference and assumption. The meanings they attach to their experiences are not necessarily the meanings that their teachers or parents would ascribe; the subcultures that children inhabit in classrooms or schools are not always visible or accessible to adults. (p.61)

They argue that there is a dominant ideology that constructs children as subjects of adult protection who are submitted to 'serious, controlled forms of socialization' (p.63). Thus schools are institutions that are broadly focused on control and domination. It is arguable that in the United Kingdom there is a cultural obsession with children and young people's behaviour that is reflected in the mass media. The introduction of Anti-Social Behaviour Orders (ASBOs) in 1999, which have been issued in increasing numbers, (Home Office Research Development and Statistics 2009) suggests that there are powerful cultural influences centred on notions of the control and submission of young people. A sociological perspective is useful as it provides a solid basis for enquiry. If children and young people are constructing their own meanings, what are they? If the notion of an ideological construction of childhood based on adults having to control children is valid, then what is it like for children who challenge this control either consciously or unwittingly?

Armstrong and Galloway (1996) argue that 'the application of expert knowledge to the care and control of children has been a major phenomenon of the twentieth century' (p.109). Their research revealed that, despite the recommendation in the original SEN Code of Practice (DfE 1994) that children be involved in decisions about assessment, monitoring and review of their special educational needs, in reality the process rarely allowed for children to express their views. They question the assumption that professionals are expressing 'disinterested concern' when referrals are made for assessment, particularly for emotional and behavioural difficulties. Their findings that the children felt uninvolved with the process suggests that whilst UK government policy appears to support the principle that children have a right to be listened to, in practice this is not occurring. Given that a Statement of Special Educational Needs can have a significant impact on a pupil's self-image (Wearmouth 1999), it would seem ethically essential to seek out the voice of the child.

The revised Code of Practice (DfES 2001) made consultation with children a fundamental principle, stating that 'the views of the child should be sought and taken into account' (1.5). However, it is important to be aware, as Davies (2005) points out, that the Code of Practice in the UK is not statutory. A current research project I am undertaking so far suggests that the consultation process is not experienced by children as an opportunity to express their views. Representative comments made by pupils with Statements for SEBD include:

> I don't go to my review meetings – I used to go and people just told me about what I'd done, and I knew about that already, so I stopped going. (Year 10 boy)

> I don't go to my review meetings 'cos I know what they're going to say, they're going to say I've got even worse and I have to calm it down but I can't. (Year 11 girl)

Unless the views of the pupils who challenge mainstream school systems, as children with SEBD tend to (Ofsted 2004), are listened to and taken into account, it is likely that their negative experiences will be perpetuated (Davies 2005).

Ethically it is essential that pupil perspectives are sought, not just for the sake of the pupils themselves, but also for the staff who are working with them. Cooper (2001) refers to the prolonged feelings of concern aroused by the behaviour of children with SEBD. Shearman (2003) describes staff feeling 'a sense of outrage that their skills are being effectively rubbished by children with (S)EBD' (p.63). This outrage can be alleviated if some understanding of why these pupils behave in the *way* they do can be developed by listening to their explanations and narratives about their behaviour.

If it is accepted that children with SEBD present difficulties for staff in schools, and that the children are responding to their environment in a way that makes sense to them, '[i]t is probably axiomatic that children to whom the descriptor (S)EBD is applied have developed ways of coping which appear from the outside to be dysfunctional but which offer for them the best or only way of dealing with a situation' (Bowers 1996, p.10). Then, it is ethically essential to discover how the children perceive their situation, both to protect their rights and to inform staff so that they too can be empowered to enable the children to cope in ways which they can work with.

Practical reasons

In 1999 I carried out a small-scale research project which explored the perceptions of Year 11 pupils who attended off-site centres in England about their quality of education (Toynbee 1999). The study sought to discover whether the pupils felt disadvantaged or stigmatised by their placement in segregated provision. The participants in the research described their educational experience in off-site centres very positively. Like Cooper's (1993a) respondents in specialist provision, they felt their relationships with staff and other pupils as well as their educational opportunities had been enhanced by their attendance at off-site centres. The experiences described matched my own assumptions as the former head teacher of one of these centres. However, when asked if there were anything they would now change about their educational histories, nine out of the fourteen participants asserted that they wished they had completed their education in mainstream schools. This seemed remarkable given the negative way in which they had described their experiences in mainstream schools and the real sense of achievement they reported in their off-site centres. This underlines the point that as researchers and classroom practitioners, we tend to see only a small part of the picture when we assume that we understand what school means to our pupils. I had completely underestimated the social importance of attending mainstream school for pupils: 'I feel like I can't fit in with some of my friends when they talk about school...they're all having fun and I'm not part of it' (Toynbee 1999, p.82). Pupil perspective research provides an essential part of the jigsaw in our attempts to make effective and positive provision for young people described as experiencing SEBD.

There is a growing body of pupil perspective literature that reveals that while policy and practice is being developed with the best interests of the children in mind, in reality it can be experienced quite differently by pupils. For example, Sinclair Taylor's (1995) study of a unit placed in the heart of an English mainstream school, with the explicit policy of enabling pupils with Statements of Special Educational Needs to integrate with their mainstream peers, was experienced by the unit pupils as stigmatising and excluding. While her research participants saw their unit as a place of sanctuary, they were also being labelled as 'dunces' by their peers. Taylor concludes: 'Evaluation of policy and practice needs to place pupils centre stage, if education is to develop responsively' (p.84).

Garner (1995) argues that:

> by offering disruptive pupils the opportunity to present their views, the 'reality gap' between what these pupils think, and what teachers and others think they think, can be significantly closed. By doing this, disruptive pupils can be viewed as resources for professional and institutional development. (p.20)

This would seem to parallel Ainscow's (1995) ideas about children with SEN providing vital feedback to schools in order for schools to develop reflective and inclusive culture and practice. Garner's (1995) study found that a significant minority of the pupils identified as disruptive largely supported wider school values; but he also found that there was a 'significant gap' between what schools claimed to provide and what pupils received. He argues that this could be used as a springboard for school improvement.

The practical reasons for consulting children experiencing SEBD centre on the idea that as adults and professionals we experience school differently from pupils. Pupils can give us significant feedback about how they experience policy and provision. Pupils with SEBD can provide us essential information about how their behaviour and responses to school make sense to them, in order that we can develop a better understanding of their needs. Garner (1995) argues that we should not extrapolate too much from small-scale studies, as this tends to put pupil views in the background. It may be argued, however, that if individual narratives are foregrounded and given authentic expression, then wider understanding of children who struggle can be developed.

Recent figures suggest that approximately 17,500 children with Statements for SEBD are being educated in mainstream primary and secondary schools in the UK.(DCSF 2008) While there are studies of pupils' perceptions of exclusion (de Pear 1997; Garner 1996; John 1996) and of pupils' experiences in specialist, segregated provision (Cooper 1993a; Howe 1995; Polat and Farrel 2002), there are few studies on pupils' perception of mainstream education from the perspective of a child identified as having SEBD (e.g. Allan

1999; Turner 2000). Given that the majority of pupils who are described as having SEBD are being educated in mainstream schools (DCSF 2008), it would seem to be relevant to explore their perception of their educational experience. It is essential to discover what aspects of mainstream schools are of importance to pupils who have been identified as struggling within the system. Wise (2000) highlighted some of the difficulties experienced by her research participants (pupils with SEBD) in mainstream schools that had ultimately led to them being unable to access mainstream school successfully. The size and layout of schools and difficulties with relationships with peers and teachers combined effectively to 'disable' these children, who ended up receiving their education outside mainstream.

The practical reasons for seeking children's views given by Lloyd-Smith and Tarr (2000) give a clear indication of how this kind of research could be valuable:

> There is (also) a role for educational research to demonstrate the potency and value of listening to children in the evaluation of national policy, the promotion of school improvement and the monitoring of provision for vulnerable and excluded groups. (p.70)

Cooper (1993b) also emphasises the importance of pupil perspectives because 'it can help us to understand the effects and evaluate the effectiveness of provision and intervention' (p.129).

While Wise (2000) subscribes to these practical considerations, she queries whether pupil perceptions can actually have an impact on policy or provision. She argues that even when pupil accounts of their schooling are believed, their views are not accorded the status of professional perceptions:

> It would seem that even if we accept the subjective reality of our pupils as being of value and not false or distorted in some way, then we must be prepared to consider them equally as clients within the system, along with professionals, parents and schools. (p.16)

This would require a significant shift in power relations described by Lloyd-Smith and Tarr (2000) as a 'vast conceptual leap' that would reconstruct children as participants rather than subjects of adult control. Some pupil perception research (e.g. Sinclair Taylor 1995) has revealed that practice intended to enact a particular policy, in this case inclusion, has had the opposite effect on pupils.

Educational interventions designed to meet the needs of young people with SEBD thus need to be examined through the eyes of the pupils for whom they are intended. This has practical value for the staff themselves. If staff in schools can develop knowledge and understanding of how behaviour that challenges and undermines adult authority makes sense to the pupils themselves, then they can respond in ways that meet the need being expressed, without perpetuating the negative behaviour. Evidence from pupil perspectives of teachers suggests that the way in which teachers respond is critical.

> [Pupils] construe identities for teachers on an individualized basis as opposed to generating a collective identity. Such identities are crucial in the way they subsequently interact with teachers and in the degree to which teachers respond thereby helping to support or frustrate development and change. (Davies 2005, p.306)

This individualisation of teachers can be seen as empowering, as it means that each teacher can make their own changes in the way they listen to and support their pupils. Professional effectiveness will be enhanced if teachers can see themselves as powerful agents in the experience that their pupils have in school. Thus, while there may be critiques of a rigid and inflexible curriculum as a contributory factor to behaviour difficulties (Fogell and Long 1997, Hamill and Boyd 2002), as individuals, teachers can adapt and deliver it in ways that can meet the needs of *all* their pupils. The teaching styles used and relationships developed between teachers and pupils then become central to successful practice. Thus, practically, listening to pupils becomes essential in the development of professional effectiveness.

CONCLUSION

In this chapter, the epistemological, ethical and practical reasons for seeking pupil perspectives have been discussed. It has been argued that children do have valuable information to share with adults, that children do have a right to have their voices heard, and that adults' views of what the experience of school is like for children needs to be examined. Children experiencing SEBD have views of particular value to contribute as it is these children who present some of the most potent challenges to mainstream schools (Ofsted 2004). It has also been argued that from a constructivist perspective the meanings made by adults and children within a school may be quite different, and that the possibilities for misunderstandings and partial knowledge without consulting all the actors within the school context are many and complex. As an example, Sinclair Taylor's (1995) research was referred to as a particularly illuminating example of the differences in the ways in which policy is enacted and experienced. The highly contested notion of inclusion has been a focus of this chapter as it is within this discourse that the voice of pupils with SEBD has rarely been heard.

My current research attempts to redress this imbalance by seeking the views of children with SEBD attending mainstream schools. Their views about inclusion, their feelings of belonging and their sense of how they feel about being identified as having SEBD have been sought. Preliminary findings suggest that attending mainstream school is extremely important from the pupil perspective. It appears that the social benefits of mainstream school attendance may be underestimated within the professional discourse about education. Thus, the target-driven attainment agenda, which informs much of the debate and discussion about quality of education, seems to be utterly irrelevant to the pupils within mainstream who are most likely to challenge the authorities within the institution. In common with Garner's (1995) findings, the pupils in the current study were broadly supportive, in theory, of mainstream school values. However, of greater importance to the participants is the loyalty to peer relationships, built up over years, that are highly significant and of great value to the pupils. Whilst this research is in the early stages of analysis, what it suggests is that pupils with SEBD can provide important evidence in the development of effective policy and practice. If what pupils consider significant is foregrounded, then evaluating policy and practice becomes rooted in a more lucid, holistic context of multiple understandings.

As researcher/practitioners we need to link differing perspectives in order to develop deeper and more complex understandings of the processes within schools. Those of us who have a particular concern for pupils with SEBD, need to highlight the significance of their perspectives in order to enable us to develop appropriate and helpful contexts in which all pupils can thrive. As Davies (2005) argues, the assumption that children with SEBD are 'almost entirely oppositional' to schools and teachers is challenged if the views of these children are actually examined. There is an increasing body of research suggesting that this assumption about the oppositional attitude of children with SEBD is exaggerated. Clearly, children and young persons can offer us a richly textured and fascinating critique of educational institutions which can enable us to develop a broader, multi-faceted understanding of the complexities, successes and shortcomings in our practice.

REFERENCES

Ainscow, M. (1995) 'Education for all: making it happen.' *Support for Learning 10*, 4, 147–154.

Allan, J. (1999) *Actively Seeking Inclusion: Pupils with Special Needs in Mainstream Schools.* London: Falmer.

Armstrong, D. and Galloway, D. (1996) 'How Children with Emotional and Behavioural Difficulties View Professionals.' In R. Davie and D. Galloway (eds) *Listening to Children in Education.* London: David Fulton.

Bowers, T. (1996) 'Putting the "E" back in EBD.' *Emotional and Behavioural Difficulties 1*, 1, 8–13.

Clark, C., Dyson, A., Millward, A. and Robson, S. (1999) 'Theories of inclusion, theories of schools: Deconstructing and reconstructing the inclusive school.' *British Educational Research Journal 25*, 2, 157–177.

Cooper, P. (1993a) *Effective Schools for Disaffected Students: Integration and Segregation.* London: Routledge.

Cooper, P. (1993b) 'Learning from pupils' perspectives.' *British Journal of Special Education 20*, 4, 129–132.

Cooper, P. (2001) *We Can Work It Out. What Works in Education for Pupils with Social, Emotional and Behavioural Difficulties Outside Mainstream Classrooms?* Ilford: Barnardo's.

Cooper, P. (2003) 'Including students with SEBD in mainstream secondary schools.' *Emotional and Behavioural Difficulties 8*, 1, 5–7.

Davies, J.D. (2005) 'Voices from the Margin: The Perceptions of Pupils with Emotional and Behavioural Difficulties about their Educational Experiences.' In P. Clough, P. Garner, J.F. Pardeck and F. Yuen (eds) *Handbook of Emotional and Behavioural Difficulties.* London: Sage.

Department for Children, Schools and Families (DCSF) (2008) Statistical First Release. Special Educational Needs in England. Available at www.dcsf.gov.uk/rsgateway/DB/SFR-2008, accessed on 7 March 2009.

Department for Education (DfE) (1994) *Code of Practice on the Identification and Assessment of Special Educational Needs.* London: DfE.

Department for Education and Science (DfES) (2001) *Special Educational Needs: Code of Practice.* London: DfES.

de Pear, S. (1997) 'Excluded pupils' views of their needs and experiences.' *Support for Learning 12*, 1, 19–22.

Fogell, J. and Long, R. (1997) *Spotlight on Special Educational Needs – Emotional and Behavioural Difficulties.* Tamworth: NASEN.

Garner, P. (1995) 'Schools by Scoundrels: The Views of "Disruptive" Pupils in Mainstream Schools in England and the United States.' In M. Lloyd-Smith and J.D. Davies (eds) *On the Margins. The Educational Experience of 'Problem' Pupils.* Chester: Trentham Books.

Garner, P. (1996) 'A la recherche du temps perdu: Case study evidence from off-site and Pupil Referral Units.' *Children and Society 10*, 187–196.

Hamill, P. and Boyd, B. (2002) 'Equality, fairness and rights – the young person's voice.' *British Journal of Special Education 29*, 3, 111–117.

Home Office Research Development and Statistics (2009) available at www.crimereduction.go.uk accessed 2 February 2009.

Howe, T. (1995) 'Former Pupils' Reflections on Residential Provision.' In M. Lloyd-Smith and J.D. Davies (eds) (1995) *On the Margins: The Educational Experience of Problem Pupils.* Chester: Trentham Books.

John, P. (1996) 'Damaged Goods? An Interpretation of Excluded Pupils' Perceptions of Schooling.' In E. Blythe and J. Milner (eds) *Exclusion from School: Interprofessional Issues for Policy and Practice.* London: Routledge.

Lloyd-Smith, M. and Tarr, J. (2000) 'Researching Children's Perspectives: A Sociological Dimension.' In A. Lewis and G. Lindsay (eds) *Researching Children's Perspectives.* Buckingham: Open University Press.

Office for Standards in Education (Ofsted) (2004) *Special Educational Needs and Disability: Towards Inclusive Schools.* London: Ofsted.

Polat, F. and Farrel, P. (2002) 'What was it like for you? Former pupils' reflections on a residential school for pupils with emotional and behavioural difficulties.' *Emotional and Behavioural Difficulties 7*, 2, 97–108.

Shearman, S. (2003) 'What is the reality of "inclusion" for children in the primary classroom?' *Emotional and Behavioural Difficulties 8*, 1, 53–76.

Sinclair Taylor, A. (1995) 'A "Dunces Place": Pupils' Perceptions of the Role of a Special Unit.' In M. Lloyd Smith and J.D. Davies (eds) *On the Margins: The Educational Experience of Problem Pupils.* Chester: Trentham Books.

Toynbee, F. (1999) *'I've learned the value of people'. Pupil Perspectives of Off-site Education.* Unpublished MA dissertation. Institute of Education, University of London.

Turner, C. (2000) 'A pupil with EBD's perspective: Does John feel that his behaviour is affecting his learning?' *Emotional and Behavioural Difficulties 5*, 4, 13–18.

Wearmouth, J. (1999) 'Another one flew over: "Maladjusted" Jack's perception of his label.' *British Journal of Special Education 26*, 1, 15–22.

Wise, S. (2000) *Listen to Me!* Bristol: Lucky Duck.

CHAPTER 3

The Narratives of Secondary School Students with SEBD

Carmel Cefai and Paul Cooper

INTRODUCTION

The UN Convention on the Rights of the Child published in 1989 has provided the impetus for the movement for the inclusion and recognition of children's voices in various contexts such as education. Legislation and policies, such as the SEN Code of Practice (DfES 2001), the Children Act 2004 and the guidelines *Working Together: Giving Children and Young People a Say* (DfES 2004) in the UK, and the National Minimum Curriculum (Ministry of Education 1999) and the Inclusive Education Policy Guidelines (Bartolo *et al.* 2002) in Malta, have underlined the need to listen to students in the various aspects of their educational experience and encourage them to participate actively in their education. Student voice is indeed driving many educational initiatives and policies, as well as the process of school development and evaluation (DfES 2002; Flutter and Rudduck 2004). These legislative and policy developments have given rise to student voice in research, with a particular focus on pupils' perceptions of their school experiences as a means of incorporating their views in issues relating to the improvement of learning and behaviour in school.

Research evidence has repeatedly underlined the fundamental differences between students' and teachers' views on various aspects of the learning experience (Garner 1995; Spera and Wentzel 2003; Wood 2003). These differences are evident amongst various groups of students, but they are particularly striking amongst students with social, emotional and behaviour difficulties (SEBD), usually the most disenfranchised and disempowered group of students. While teachers may complain about lack of motivation, defiance and disruption of lessons, students may regard such behaviours as appropriate ways to solve problems or as a response to poor teaching or unfair treatment (Clark *et al.* 2005; Cooper and McIntyre 1993; Riley 2004). Students' complaints about a boring and irrelevant curriculum may be considered by teachers as a sign of their unwillingness to 'co-operate' or inability to learn (Chircop 1997). In a qualitative study carried out in a Welsh primary school with a considerable number of pupils with behaviour problems, the teachers blamed the pupils' personality and temperament, difficulties in coping with work, attention seeking, and family problems as being the main causes of misbehaviour. The pupils on the other hand mentioned school factors (teasing and bullying by peers, teachers' attitude, and learning difficulties) as significant causes of their difficulties (Cefai 1995).

The differences between teachers' and students' perspectives underline the need to engage students in dialogue and give them a valid, 'warranting voice' (Gergen 2001). What students with SEBD have to say about their learning and behaviour at school is not only valid and meaningful but helps to provide a more adequate and useful construction of the situation, contributing to a better understanding and resolution of difficulties. They are able to throw light upon the causes and nature of learning and behaviour difficulties which might be overlooked or not mentioned by teachers (Hamill and Boyd 2002; Rudduck 2002; Fielding and Bragg, 2003). Cooper (1996) argues that students should be seen as a source of knowledge and expertise, having unique inside experience of what it is like to be a student in a particular school. Their views help to throw light on what school practices and conditions may lead to a sense of helplessness and alienation, or conversely facilitate their learning and make them feel valued as members of their community (Cooper 2003; Ruddock and Flutter 2000). They are also able to provide an accurate account of their own learning processes and how these could be enhanced by classroom teaching practices (Cooper and McIntyre 1993). Besides helping adults to develop insights about the nature, cause and resolution of challenging behaviour, giving students the opportunity to discuss and express their views provides them with an opportunity to gain an insight into their own behaviour and its influence on their own and others' learning and relationships. This helps to prevent feelings of helplessness and alienation and empowers the students to take more control and responsibility for their own behaviour and behaviour change (Hapner and Imel 2002; Kroeger *et al.* 2004; Norwich and Kelly 2006).

Clearly, the inclusion of the student perspective helps to promote more effective learning and positive behaviour in school. Yet the inclusion of the perspectives of students with SEBD in school is quite a recent phenomenon and in many schools the opportunities for such students to make their voices heard are still very limited. Although the National Minimum Curriculum in Malta promotes democratic schools as one of its key principles, students' participation in decisions is still largely cosmetic with most of the decisions in schools being made by adults (Cefai 2007). Student councils are being set up in many primary and secondary schools, but their development in terms of real influence on issues that matter is still at a very early stage. Moreover as Whitty and Wisby (2007) argue, schools must seek to include the voice of all their students, not just those on a school council or who are most comfortable expressing their views in a school context. They suggest approaches which combine 'representative' and more 'participatory' forms of democracy, accommodating a wide range of abilities and disabilities. This would include students with SEBD, usually the least empowered and liked group of students (Cooper 2006; Lewis and Burman 2008). This chapter presents a review of a number of recent studies carried out with Maltese students with SEBD exploring their views on various facets of their educational experience. The scarcity of research available in this area reflects the actual lack of attention given to the student voice, particularly those with SEBD, in school.

THE VOICE OF STUDENTS WITH SEBD IN MALTESE SCHOOLS

In a recent national study on students with social, emotional and behaviour difficulties in Malta, taking 10 per cent of the school population across the primary and secondary school levels, it was found that according to teachers, 9.7 per cent of the students exhibit social, emotional and behaviour difficulties (Cefai, Cooper and Camilleri 2008). As expected, there are more difficulties in secondary than primary schools, with difficulties increasing as students move from primary to secondary education, especially behavioural problems. Boys were reported to have more difficulties than girls (10.46% and 8.86% respectively), and while they exhibited more behaviour problems, emotional difficulties were more prevalent amongst female students. The great majority of these students are supported in the mainstream, with only about 0.2 per cent of students with SEBD attending special schools or units (Cefai and Cooper 2006). The 9.7 per cent prevalence rate is close to the 10 per cent rate given by Robert Goodman (Goodman 1997) and other studies based on teacher perceptions (Egelund and Hansen 2000; Smeets et al. 2007), but lower than the

10–20 per cent rate suggested by other researchers in the UK (BMA 2006; Young Minds 1999). The Maltese study suggested that local statistics are quite close to the international prevalence rates, and that teacher responses strongly indicate that SEBD are a major issue of concern in Maltese schools.

A preliminary search for local studies on the voice of students with SEBD yielded a very small number of small-scale studies carried out in the past decade or so with secondary school students. Table 3.1 gives a brief description of the studies reviewed in this chapter. The studies have been all undertaken with secondary school students or students who had finished school, and they have all included students identified as having SEBD, namely students with behaviour difficulties in mainstream secondary schools or in special schools, and students who were regular absentees (not for medical reasons). All the studies included interviews with the students about their mainstream school experiences. Students attributed their difficulties, disaffection and disengagement to a combination of school and out-of-school factors, but this chapter will focus on the school-related factors referred to by the students. Five major common themes were identified in the narratives of the participants with regards to their mainstream educational experiences and their consequent disengagement, namely:

- poor relationships with teachers
- victimisation by staff and peers
- oppression and powerlessness
- unconnected learning experiences
- exclusion and stigmatisation.

Poor relationships with teachers

One of the most common and frequently mentioned grievances by the students across the various studies was the perceived lack of respect, under-standing and support by their classroom teachers. Teachers failed to appreciate and address their needs, and this was a major factor that contributed to their learning and behaviour problems. They felt humiliated and inadequate when teachers shouted at them in front of their peers, ignored them or refused to listen to their views, and did not provide support with their learning diffi-culties:

> Certain teachers start shouting at you when you say something...for example if you go near the teacher and tell him 'Good morning', he tells you that he has no time to waste. Or you go near some other teacher and ask for help with work and she tells you 'You did not pay attention' ...or

Table 3.1: Studies on students with SEBD in Maltese schools						
Authors	Participants	Age	Number	Gender	Method	Analysis
Massa (2002)	Secondary school students with SEBD	11–13	8	Mixed	Semi-structured interviews	Thematic analysis
Bartolo and Tabone (2002)	Secondary school students with SEBD	11–14	20	Mixed	Semi-structured interviews	Thematic analysis
Dalli and Dimech (2005)	Secondary school students with SEBD, including excluded and frequent absentees	11–16	19	Girls	Participant observation, semi-structured interviews	Ethnographic Feminist/ critical theory analysis
Spiteri (2009)	Ex SEBD school students	16 yrs+	12	Boys	Unstructured interviews	Grounded theory analysis
Chircop (1997)	Trade school habitual absentees	15–16	15	Girls	Participant observation, semi-structured interviews	Grounded theory analysis
Clark et al. (2005)	Secondary school regular absentees	14–16	25	Mixed	Focus groups	Thematic analysis
Gonzi et al. (2006)	Young persons attending services or schools for young persons with challenging behaviour	14–18	14	Mixed	Semi-structured interviews	Thematic analysis

you say something and he tells you 'You do not understand...' (Jane) (Massa 2002)

If they (teachers) listen more, we wouldn't get so angry and we wouldn't get in trouble as much; the few times we were given a say about a particular behaviour incident or we just decided to speak up, we were either ignored or not believed. (Ramona) (Bartolo and Tabone 2002)

Ramona was more specific on what teacher behaviours will help her improve her behaviour:

My behaviour would improve if the teacher doesn't always come angry for the lesson...and if they are more friendly...I behave well with those [teachers] who love me and bad with those who don't.

The students said they did not feel close enough to disclose personal problems with their classroom teachers. Anna who has since left school, describes how upset she was when her teacher broke the trust she (Anna) had put in her:

> But then they amplify [things]…why disclose with all the class that problem which I came to tell you?…if so, then it's worth telling the whole class myself, because they will get to know anyway…a girl from my class would know; some 10 other girls from other classes, she'd go and tell them, and those will go and tell another 10 girls and then the word is spread around the whole school. Anna here and Anna there and everyone gossiping about me. (Gonzi *et al.* 2006)

On the other hand, when teachers were understanding and took time to listen to the students and their difficulties, the students felt comfortable and accepted, and had no problems in engaging with what was taking place in the classroom:

> She gives you attention…if she sees that you are unhappy she asks you if she can do anything to help…sometimes during a lesson she tells us 'I have been talking so much that I must have given you a headache' and she tells us a joke… (Jane) (Massa 2002)

> Not all teachers are negative. There is one I really like…has a very nice character. For example I confide with her when I have personal problems and she listens to me and respects me. (Berta) (Clark *et al.* 2005)

Andrew had a negative experience in the mainstream, but he found respite, care and understanding in his present special school for young persons with challenging behaviour:

> [I am] very happy because they teach me and listen to me…I am learning to write bit by bit and – they understand me and do not send me away and shout at me. (Gonzi *et al.* 2006)

Clearly when students felt listened to and understood and treated with respect and care they were more willing to make an effort to improve their behaviour and engage in the classroom activities. The close relationship with the teachers provided a scaffold that helped them to find stability in a sometimes disorganised and chaotic life, to believe in themselves, and to find meaning in their school experiences.

  A related subtheme across the studies was the autocratic and rigid behaviour management approach adopted by many teachers in their response to misbehaviour. Their blaming and punitive approach based on control and coercion was seen in many cases as leading to an exacerbation and worsening of the problem. Jane mentioned how many of her teachers 'were not calm and did not know how to joke' (Massa 2002), Patricia complains about being used 'as an example for the class...' (Dalli and Dimech 2005), while Ramona describes how her English teacher 'makes her mad':

> The teacher is too strict...I don't like it when they are like this, so I get more mad in their lessons... I misbehave because they make me mad. (Bartolo and Tabone 2002)

> They only get angry. I only wanted her to help me but she started shouting at me right away. (Rebecca) (Bartolo and Tabone 2002)

The way the teachers handled the situation would thus lead to a power struggle spiralling out of control. Andrew remarked how his school experience was a positive one, until in Year 3 in primary school, a 'harsh teacher' triggered a downward spiral and he started falling behind, leading to his eventual exclusion from school (Gonzi *et al.* 2006). Maria, a student with behaviour problems, remarked how being picked upon repeatedly by the teacher led her to 'pester' the teacher and 'disrupt her lesson in revenge' (Dalli and Dimech 2005). Simone who became a habitual absentee in the secondary school describes the following incident:

> There was a teacher who was always sending me to the Head office. All the time going up and down. And then I used to tease her of having a squint when I returned. And I used to eat with my feet on the table. (Clarke *et al.* 2005)

Victimisation by staff and peers

Being treated unfairly and picked on by teachers and peers was another major cause for concern expressed by students across the studies. Angela's complaint epitomises the sense of injustice felt by the students: 'Do you know what bothers me here? The teachers blame everything that happens on me' (Clark *et al.* 2005). Students defended their behaviour as a rightful and justified reaction to what they regarded as unfair treatment by teachers. They felt hurt and angry when they were singled out for misbehaviour while others got away with it, and even more when they got blamed and punished for their peers' behaviour without the teachers even bothering to verify the facts:

> So many of the others break rules and get away but I always get punished... Sometimes I get into trouble because my friends do something wrong and the teacher blames me and yells at me... When they are not fair, I get angry and I don't listen to them...I answer back...but

when they have a good reason I stay quiet. (Ramona) (Bartolo and Tabone 2002)

I stay with two other girls, he always pick on us three, he reports us for nothing, if he does not manage to finish the lesson, he blames us three for it. (Jennifer) (Massa 2002)

Patricia expresses her irritation and bitterness at the perceived injustice:

He puts up a scene for the least reason; they set you up as an example to others... [addressing one of the teachers] As long as Brenda is paying attention, you don't really care. She's the one you dedicate all your efforts to. (Dalli and Dimech 2005)

These negative experiences evoked very strong negative emotions even after the students had stopped going to school. Jason, a young person who attends a special school for behaviour difficulties, was very unhappy in the mainstream secondary and explains his outbursts, and consequent absenteeism, on the basis of unfair treatment by teachers:

I was very unhappy there...the 'sir' would make me lose my temper and then I'd throw a table at him...for example he would give written work of one kind to the other students, but then would give me written work just for me...to me and to someone else sitting in my bench. (Clark *et al.* 2005)

Bullying and teasing by peers added to the sense of victimisation experienced by students with SEBD. The students felt threatened and unsafe, frequently picked on by peers with little support from the staff. This led them frequently into trouble with both peers and staff and in many cases ending up in isolation and absenteeism. Schooling came to be perceived as a negative, destructive experience with frequent physical and psychological bullying:

Sometimes they make me very angry...and I hit them...but it's not my fault. They pick on me and I don't do anything to them... How long am I going to keep on letting them do that? (being hit) (Simon) (Bartolo and Tabone 2002)

That my father was a heavy drinker...(the other students used to say): 'You beaten one, where is the drunk? Drunkard!' ...I always went on keeping it all inside. (Anna) (Gonzi *et al.* 2005)

Over there (at the mainstream school), they used to call me names time and time over. As a result of what they used to call me, I went through a crisis. I wanted to be liked by my friends. Yet, they kept on calling me girlish. (Gilbert) (Spiteri 2009)

Oppression and powerlessness

The students felt they could do little at the school to change their predicament and get respite from their daily hassles. As one student put it 'The teacher makes the rules' (Bartolo and Tabone 2002). A sense of helplessness underlined their grievance that they had little or no say at the school, with the teachers and administration wielding the authority and making decisions without consultation. They formed part of an oppressive, undemocratic system built on adult power, compliance and coercion with little dialogue or sharing of responsibility; this left them alienated and led them to disengage from the system (Clark *et al.* 2005; Dalli and Dimech 2005). As Carmen, a 15-year-old girl who has stopped going to school, put it 'School is like a prison to me' (Chircop 1997). As described earlier, the way teachers dealt with challenging behaviour was described by many of the students across the studies as being autocratic and unfair, leaving them with no option but to fight the system or disengage from it.

> I did not want to learn the stuff they were trying to teach me at the secondary school...who gave the right to the teachers to try to force me to learn things? (Pierre) (Spiteri 2009)

> The never ask us – they just say you can't talk, eat and things like that. There is no discussion. (Tracy) (Bartolo and Tabone 2002)

> It's better if they ask us first, because we will agree more and move on...then maybe they will see that some rules are stupid... (Simone) (Bartolo and Tabone 2002)

A typical example was the issue of the uniform with some of the students, particularly girls. Many disliked the uniform, describing it as unattractive and uncomfortable, and engaged in various ways to modify it according to their likes. This may be described as a form of symbolic resistance to authority, part of the anti-school culture (cf. Patterson, Reid and Dishion 1992):

> I don't like tight pants; what difference does it make if our pants have slits? It's stupid...and I will open them again because I don't like it...it doesn't make sense. (Simone) (Bartolo and Tabone 2002)

> I really disliked having to take off the earrings...the summer one [uniform] is like a napkin, the winter one carnival. (Simone) (Clark *et al.* 2005)

The students would appreciate more consideration of their opinions and believe this would help improve both their learning (as teachers would know what helps or hinders students from learning) and their behaviour (as students are treated with respect and responsibility) (Bartolo and Tabone 2002; Dalli and Dimech 2005; Massa 2002):

> We can fix things in the school if they listen to us more. The teachers don't know everything…I think we have good ideas (Bartolo and Tabone 2002)

> If they ask what we like in the lessons, we won't get bored (because) they will do what we…enjoy…and not what they want all the time. … We know what we like and maybe we will learn more if they do this. (Bartolo and Tabone 2002)

The issue of oppression was also evident in the way some students saw an imposition of the alien school culture on their own. They sought to resist the attempts of enculturation by refusing the values projected by the school, such as behaving and dressing in ways which conflicted with the culture in their communities and peer group (Chircop 1997; Clark *et al.* 2005). Students' behaviour is defined as being rude and lacking in moral values; in turn teachers are defined as elitist and 'know it all'. Dalli and Dimech (2005) recount an incident that illustrates this culture clash, with teachers downgrading the students' use of own dialect and putting pressure on them to switch their language code to that of the school. The teacher told a student: 'You sound like a seller at the Flea Market; at school you have to learn to speak well and not with this rude accent of yours' The student replied: 'I have talked like this since I was young; if you don't like it, lump it'. Clearly the student was arguing that her 'different' culture was valuable in equipping her to function in her own social context (Dalli and Dimech 2005).

Unconnected learning experiences

Many of the participants in the various studies found the curriculum boring and academic, unrelated to life and career. They had difficulty in engaging in activities that seemed meaningless and irrelevant to real-life situations, such as the concerns they had in their life and in their communities. Veronica put it quite succntly: 'I think that this school is useless. They don't teach. Everybody goes for a laugh (Chircop 1997). Maria found it difficult to participate when 'the lessons are useless… like the languages because sometimes you don't need them in the future, like Spanish' (Bartolo and Tabone 2002). They disliked traditional lessons based mainly on written academic work with little interaction and application to real life; they preferred to learn through practical, hands-on activities:

> I think that if we do not like writing they should teach us trades and crafts. If we do not like academic work, we can learn something else...I used to enjoy [Art], but this was given least priority as it was considered a waste of time. (Clark *et al.* 2005)

As students got older they found their own ways to subvert the system by creating their own timetable and make the school experience enjoyable and exciting through misbehaviour. Cynthia, a regular absentee, describes how 'we used to do whatever we wanted...we either didn't write, or we used to chat, depending on the mood (Chircop 1997). It looks as if there was a positive correlation between progressing from one year to the other and increasing disengagement and alienation from the mainstream curriculum, with the anti-establishment agenda and life outside school gaining more prominence and meaning in the students' lives (cf. Cooper 2003). A study carried out by the World Health Organization in a number of European countries including Malta, found an increasing loss of interest in, and sense of disenchantment with, schooling amongst students in general as they progressed from one year to the other. Liking for school decreased substantially from 11 to 13 years, namely from 30 per cent to 16 per cent amongst boys, and from 50 per cent to 27 per cent amongst girls (WHO 2008). In the case of students with SEBD, however, these are usually the ones who are most sensitive to negative elements in the school's psychosocial climate, such as unhealthy relationships, rigid regimes, and boring curricula, and the first to complain about it (Cooper 1993). The following two students seek to justify their habitual absenteeism:

> They tell me go to school so that you will find a job when you grow up, but I still found a job, I had many offers of work. There is no need to go to school to find work. (Clark *et al.* 2005)

> I come to school because I am forced to, if I was 16, I will be working, at least you get something then, but here at school you get nothing. A waste of time. (Clark *et al.* 2005)

Students are also vocal about what might have helped to remain engaged:

> If they ask what we like and have fun in the lessons, we won't get bored [because] they will do what we...enjoy...and not what they want all the time. (Bartolo and Tabone 2002)

Indeed when the subject was related to their needs and made sense, the students found the experience worthwhile. During a pastoral care lesson, students who during other lessons were described as oppositional and non-compliant, co-operated with the teacher, paid attention and participated actively and enthusiastically in the lesson (Chircop 1997).

Exclusion and stigmatisation

In more ways than one, students said that they felt excluded as schools and teachers showed an unwillingness and/or inability to understand them and repeatedly failed to accommodate to their social and emotional needs. They found it difficult to thrive in a rigid, autocratic system that expected them to change and adapt and left little space for flexibility and autonomy. As mentioned earlier on, this inflexibility and lack of understanding and support made it impossible for students with particular social and emotional needs to succeed. Despite a National Minimum Curriculum promoting a policy of inclusion (Ministry of Educaiton 1999), this was one of the groups of students with individual educational needs with whom schools found it most difficult to move from principle and rhetoric to actual practice. Indeed the SEBD group is at the greatest risk of exclusion, it being the only group where punitive, exclusionary responses are permitted by law (Cooper 2001). They are usually the least liked and understood students, with teachers preferring other students in their classroom, including those with severe intellectual disability or learning difficulties (Baker 2005).

Students said that their learning needs were similarly not being addressed, compounding their existing problems at school. Not getting support when needing help in learning led to boredom and frustration and consequently misbehaviour.

> We don't understand and they do not explain to us and this annoys me. (Janet) (Dalli and Dimech 2005)

> We had a comprehension exercise and I was reading while she was explaining because it was difficult and she gave me a detention. (Rianne) (Massa 2002)

In such circumstances students are likely to find themselves victims of labelling and stigmatisation. The label they end up with as a result of lack of support to their educational needs ('failure', 'incompetent', 'unmotivated'), in turn leads to a self-fulfilling prophecy where the students stop believing in themselves, take the label assigned to them and start calling themselves stupid, inadequate and failures

> I'm good for nothing. They tell me I'm spaced out.

> It is useless sir when you [I] are incapable of understanding; I am not sitting for any O levels because it's useless for me to do so; I'm not up to standard...a waste of money. (Dalli and Dimech 2005)

This process is set to lead to disengagement and consequent misbehaviour and absenteeism as students try to detach themselves from a system that has a very negative effective on their view of themselves in such a delicate and vulnerable time in their development. Seen in this way, disengagement becomes a self-protective mechanism from an act of symbolic violence by an inhuman, uncaring system (Chircop 1997).

ANALYSIS

Students with SEBD, including those who still attended mainstream schools, those who were placed at special schools/units, and those who had stopped attending school, described their mainstream school experience as an unpleasant and unhappy one. Not only did they feel cheated by not receiving the support they needed in their learning and in their socio-emotional development, but they felt victimised and abused by a system that labelled them as deviant and failures, putting them even more at risk for social exclusion as young adults. They protested against a system that was exclusive and discriminative, failing to address and accommodate their needs and labelling them instead as difficult and antisocial. This had a negative impact on their self-esteem at a critical stage in their development, sometimes leading to a self-fulfilling prophecy where the students themselves started to doubt their own capabilities and resources to face the challenges as young adults in society.

The students felt isolated and victimised by inflexible teachers and bullying peers. They felt particularly vulnerable when teachers failed to understand them and their needs and refused to listen to them and their concerns. They had no say in what was happening at the school or in the classroom, and in many instances were not given the opportunity to defend themselves in episodes of behaviour difficulties; in some instances being unfairly punished.

Another key theme was that students found it difficult to engage in traditional, teacher-centred methods of teaching and curricula, which they saw as irrelevant to their real life and which were sometimes in conflict with the cultures of their own peer group and community. They found themselves helpless, excluded and alienated in a system marked by uncaring relationships, oppression, injustice and victimisation. Their basic psychological needs for affiliation, competence, success, achievement, autonomy and fun were clearly not addressed. In their eyes, the school experience led to their being isolated and friendless, to a sense of failure and inadequacy, and to being coerced and punished in their struggle for self-definition and autonomy.

On the other hand, the students were quite clear on what school factors would have helped them to feel happier at school and made their experience a more rewarding one. They underlined the need for a more humane, caring, inclusive, democratic and relevant system. They warmed to those teachers who showed them care and understanding, who listened to them and their concerns, and who supported them in their social and learning difficulties. They were ready to invest in teachers who respected them and believed in them despite their difficulties. They referred to the significance of caring relationships with particular teachers and the power of such relationships in realigning their development towards more positive pathways (cf. Pianta 1999). They asked for protection from an oppressive and abusive system, to be replaced by a system where they would be treated fairly without undue blame, where they would have a right of reply, and where they are not blamed and bullied. They wanted to have more say about the decisions affecting their lives. They wished that what they had to do at school made more sense to their present lives and future career prospects, and helped them to develop their strengths and talents, rather than exacerbating their weaknesses and difficulties. When they were given a second chance, such as going to another school, one which addressed their needs, they reported a more positive view of school and learning, which in turn led to more positive view of themselves and their abilities, a process Cooper (1993) calls 'positive resignification'. The following excerpts by adolescents and young adults who attended special schools (Gonzi et al. 2006, Spiteri 2009) indicate the processes that helped to re-engage the students in the educational process and start to believe again in themselves:

> Very happy [at present school] because they teach me and listen to me...I am learning to write bit by bit and – they understand me and not send me away and shout at me. (Andrew) (Gonzi et al. 2006)

> Come and enjoy it – you won't get bored here...time will pass for you over here...I don't even see the time pass by. (Jason) (Gonzi et al. 2006)

> The headmaster told me 'over here you will learn what it is that you want to learn.' There were no extra-clever students. Everyone was the same. (Pierre) (Spiteri 2009)

> For me, the most important thing is that teachers show you that they care about you and that they understand you. Today I am a mechanic. I have always wanted to be a mechanic. At school, I was allowed to dis-

mantle and reassemble parts of a broken-down car. What more could I have possibly wanted then? The teachers there gave me the courage to say this is what I want to do, and I am going to do it. (Louis) (Spiteri 2009)

The schools above helped the students to feel valued members of their community and consequently to shed their negative labels and develop more positive views of themselves. This process resonates with other similar studies carried out with students in special schools, such as those by Cooper (1993), Polat and Farrel (2002) and Jahnukainen (2001), where students were found to look at their special school as providing respite from the difficulties they encountered in their former schools, particularly unsatisfactory relationships with school staff, inconsistent and unfair treatment by staff, and inadequate personal and academic support from staff. As in the case of the various accounts described above, for many students the positive relationships they formed with the staff were seen as contributing directly to various positive outcomes in their lives, such as enhanced self-esteem and self-worth (Cooper 1993; Jahnukainen 2001).

It is more effective however, for mainstream schools to promote such positive experiences from the start and prevent negative signification from taking place (Cooper 1993). For instance, other studies have found that the students themselves would have liked to experience the positive factors present in the special school in their previous mainstream schools (Garner 1995; Gonzi et al. 2006; Toynbee 1999). Healthy student–teacher relationships, caring and supportive teachers, flexible classroom management, meaningful engagement, inclusion, and support in academic and personal needs, are processes that may be promoted in any school. Mainstream schools can help students to develop a positive identity and sense of responsibility through opportunities to feel valued, included, competent and autonomous. This will lead to more positive social and academic behaviours amongst the students (Cefai 2008).

Reading this chapter, school staff may regard it as a one-sided attack on schools and teachers by bitter and angry young people with negative school experiences. Indeed, one must be careful not to make the same mistake of previous research by focusing on the views of one party only. As already indicated, it is crucial to listen to all the views, particularly those of teachers, parents and students, in seeking to gain more adequate understandings and insights of the processes underlying student behaviour at school. It is thus important to underline that the focus taken in this chapter should not be taken to imply that the student perspective is more important or valid than those of teachers. Indeed supporting students with SEBD is a demanding and challenging task, and the teachers themselves need support in addressing the needs of such students. It is also important to mention that when asked about their school experiences, many of the students in the studies reviewed in this chapter, listed other non-school factors that contributed to their difficulties at school, such as individual characteristics, family and community problems, and peer group pressure. This chapter, however, is concerned with how listening to the students' voice can make a significant contribution to schools in their efforts to promote a more positive experience for all students, particularly vulnerable ones. The narratives of the students described above underline the benefits for school staff to listen to what students would like to see in their school and how this is related to better adjustment and success in learning. In the end this makes for effective teaching and learning (Cooper and McIntyre 1993; Hapner and Imel 2002).

CONCLUSION

Students sent out a very clear message of what processes help them to learn and engage in positive social and academic behaviour, and what they find discouraging, devaluing and disheartening. Clearly, schools need to operate as caring, inclusive and supportive communities for all their members, including those with social and emotional needs. They need to engage in more frequent and regular dialogue with the students on what is helping or hindering them from learning and make the necessary adjustments accordingly. Students with SEBD need to be given more opportunity to give their views on the various facets of their educational experiences and need to be provided with skills to enable them to do so effectively. This implies first that teachers must have a genuine desire to listen to what the students have to say. They will need to see the significance and value of eliciting students' views as a crucial element in effective teaching and behaviour management, as only then will they seek to engage in pupil consultation (McIntyre, Pedder and Rudduck 2005). Teachers will feel less threatened of 'student power' if they have clear ideas of what 'student voice' entails. It does not mean that teacher authority would be taken over by the students, or as Nieto (1994, p.398) put it, that students would have the 'final and conclusive word in how schools need to change'. Rather it is a dialogue between students and teachers, with the latter considering and incorporating students' views when making classroom decisions. Teachers will also need to appreciate that by giving students a voice, their relationships with the students would improve, as the dialogue between teachers and students would help to break down barriers and build connections. The students will stop blaming the school for their problems, and as their sense of helplessness and oppression decreases, their sense of responsibility will increase (Fielding and Bragg 2003; McBeath 2006). They would thus have no need to shout to make themselves heard.

Second, the students themselves need to be convinced that they have a valuable contribution to make. Paradoxically, the teachers themselves need to help students to challenge the notion that teachers know best and start believing more in themselves (Flutter and Rudduck 2004). Giving away their 'power' is thus set to bring the teachers closer to the students and increase their influence on student learning and behaviour. Third, schools and teachers will need to enable and support students to articulate their views as clearly and effectively as possible, particularly those who have difficulty in doing so, such as students with SEBD (Cooper 1993; Lincoln 1995). Students with SEBD may lack confidence and competence in expressing their views clearly and accurately, particularly in environments perceived as being oppressive, patronising and adult-controlled (Daniels *et al.* 2003). Indeed some of the challenging behaviour exhibited by students may be construed as an immature and unskilled way of making oneself heard. Students with SEBD may therefore need particular support, such as active listening, empathy and probing, to engage in self-reflection and insightful thinking about their experiences and to express their thoughts and reflections in appropriate, effective ways (Hapner and Imel 2002; Lincoln 1995). Fourth, there needs to be more child-friendly and emancipatory approaches to eliciting students' views so as to ensure authentic representations and constructions with the least bias and distortion. These may include strategies that promote and enhance students' active participation and communication, such as an open, non-hierarchical, facilitative and reflexive stance on the part of the adult, and child-accessible techniques that enable the children to express themselves clearly and meaningfully. Illuminative techniques such as drawings, interactive story-telling, use of pictures, sentence completion and balloon-filling, are promising tools in seeking to capture the authentic experiences of students with challenging behaviour (Wetton and Williams 2000). Rather than being the objects of research, students become partners in the research process. Finally, having a voice is not enough; students' voice needs to inform decisions and action plans. Students need not only to voice their views, concerns and suggestions, but to be actively involved in decisions and action taken to turn their voices into actual practice in the classroom (Holdsworth 2006). This would ensure that the student voice would become a vehicle for emancipation and empowerment rather than a tool for maintaining adult control.

REFERENCES

Baker, P.H. (2005) 'Managing student behaviour: How ready are teachers to meet the challenge?' *American Secondary Education 33*, 3, 50–67.

Bartolo, P., Aguis Ferrante, C., Azzopardi, A., Bason, L., Grech, L. and King, M. (2002) *Creating Inclusive Schools: Guidelines for the Implementation of the National Minimum Curriculum Policy on Inclusive Education*. Malta: Ministry of Education.

Bartolo, P. and Tabone, J. (2002) *The Voice of the Students: A Qualitative Investigation on the Views of Secondary School Students with Behaviour Problems*. Unpublished BEd (Hons) dissertation. Faculty of Education, University of Malta.

British Medical Association (2006) *Child and adolescent mental health – A Guide for Healthcare Professionals*. London: BMA.

Cefai, C. (1995) *Pupils', Parents' and Teachers' Perceptions of Behaviour Problems and School Family Interactions in a Mainstream Primary School*. Unpublished MEd dissertation. University of Wales Swansea.

Cefai, C. (2007) 'Resilience for all: A study of classrooms as protective contexts.' *Emotional and Behavioural Difficulties 12*, 2, 119–134.

Cefai, C. (2008) *Promoting Resilience in the Classroom: A Guide to Developing Emotional and Cognitive Skills*. London: Jessica Kingsley Publishers.

Cefai, C. and Cooper, P. (2006) 'Social, emotional and behavioural difficulties in Malta: An educational perspective.' *Journal of Maltese Educational Studies l*, 4, 18–36.

Cefai, C., Cooper, P. and Camilleri, L. (2008) *Engagement Time: A National Study of Students with Social, Emotional and Behaviour Difficulties in Maltese Schools*. Malta: University of Malta.

Chircop, D. (1997) 'Voting with their Feet: Students and Absenteeism.' In R. Sultana (ed) *Inside/Outside Schools: Towards a Critical Sociology of Education in Malta*. Malta: PEG Publications.

Clark, M., Borg, S., Calleja, G., Chircop, F. and Portelli, R. (2005) *School Attendance Improvement Report October 2005*. Malta: Ministry of Education, Youth and Employment.

Cooper, P. (1993) 'Learning from pupils' perspectives.' *British Journal of Special Education 20*, 4, 129–133.

Cooper, P. (1996) 'Pupils as Partners: Pupils' Contributions to the Governance of Schools.' In K. Jones and T. Charlton (editors) *Overcoming Learning and Behaviour Difficulties*. London: Routledge.

Cooper, P. (2001) *We Can Work It Out: What Works in Educating Pupils with Social, Emotional and Behavioural Difficulties: Inclusive Practice in Mainstream Schools*. London: Routledge/Falmer.

Cooper (2003) 'Including students with SEBD in mainstream secondary schools.' *Emotional and Behavioural Difficulties 8*, 1, 5–7.

Cooper, P. (2006) 'John's story: Episode 1 – Understanding SEBD from the inside: The importance of listening to young people.' In Hunter-Carsch, M., Tiknaz, Y., Cooper, P. and Sage, R. (eds) *The Handbook of Social, Emotional and Behavioural Difficulties*. London: Continuum International Publishing Group.

Cooper, P. and McIntyre, D. (1993) 'Commonality in teachers' and pupils' perceptions of effective classroom learning.' *British Journal of Educational Psychology 63*, 381–399.

Dalli, M. and Dimech, N. (2005) *A Goal to the Eye: Teacher Strategies in Dealing with Misbehaviour*. Unpublished BEd dissertation. Faculty of Education, University of Malta.

Daniels, H., Cole, T., Sellman, E., Sutton, J., Visser, J., and Bedward, J (2003) *Study of Young People Permanetly Excluded from School*. London: DfES.

Department for Education and Science (2001) *Special Educational Needs: Code of Practice*. London: DfES.

Department for Education and Science (2002) *Citizenship: The National Curriculum for England*. London: DfES.

Department for Education and Science (2004) *Working Together: Giving Children and Young People a Say*. London: DfES.

Egelund, N. and Hansen, K. (2000) 'Behavioural disorders in Danish schools: A quantitative survey.' *European Journal of Special Needs Education 15*, 2, 158–170.

Fielding, M. and Bragg, S. (2003) *Students as Researchers: Making a Difference*. Cambridge: Pearson Publishing.

Flutter, J. and Rudduck, J. (2004) *Consulting Pupils: What's in It for Schools?* London: Routledge Falmer.

Garner, P. (1995) 'Schools by Scoundrels: The Views of "Disruptive" Pupils in Mainstream Schools in England and the United States.' In M. Lloyd-Smith and J.D. Davies (eds) *On the Margins: The Educational Experience of 'Problem' Pupils*. Chester: Trentham Books.

Gergen, K.J. (2001) 'Psychological science in a postmodern world.' *American Psychologist 56*, 803–813.

Gonzi, M. *et al.* (2006) 'See Me, Listen to Me! Children's Perspectives.' In Commissioner for Children, *A Fair Deal. A Study on Children and Young People with Very Challenging Behaviour*. Office of the Commissioner for Children, Malta.

Goodman, R. (1997) 'The Strengths and Difficulties Questionnaire: A research note.' *Journal of Child Psychology and Psychiatry 38*, 581–586.

Hamill, P. and Boyd, B. (2002) 'Equality, fairness and rights – The young person's voice.' *British Journal of Special Education 29*, 3, 111–119.

Hapner, A. and Imel, B. (2002) 'The students' voice.' *Remedial and Special Education 23*, 122–127.

Holdsworth, R. (2006) *Student Action Teams: Productive Practices in Primary and Secondary Classrooms*. Melbourne: Connect Publications.

Jahnukainen, M. (2001) 'Experiencing special education: Former students of classes for the emotionally behavourally disordered talk about their schooling'. *Emotional and Behavioural Difficulties 6*, 3, 150–66.

Jones, K. and Charlton, T. (1996) 'Sources of Learning and Behaviour Difficulties.' In K. Jones and T. Charlton (eds) *Overcoming Learning and Behaviour Difficulties*. London: Routledge.

Kroeger, S., Burton, C., Comarata, A., Combs, C., Hamm, C., Hopkins, R. and Kouche, B. (2004) Student voice and critical reflection: Helping students at risk.' *Teaching Exceptional Children 36*, 3, 50–57.

Lewis, R., and Burman, E. (2008) 'Providing for student voice in classroom management: Teachers views'. *International Journal of Inclusive Education 12*, 2, 151–67.

Lincoln, Y.S. (1995) 'In search of student voices.' *Theory into Practice 34*, 2, 88–93.

MacBeath, J. (2006) 'Finding a voice, finding self'. *Educational Reviews 58*, 2, 195–207.

Massa, S. (2002) *The School as a Community: Perceptions of Secondary School Students with Emotional Behavioural Difficulties*. Unpublished BEd dissertation. Faculty of Education, University of Malta.

McIntyre, D., Pedder, D. and Rudduck, J. (2005) 'Pupil voice: Comfortable and uncomfortable learnings for teachers.' *Research Papers in Education 20*, 2, 149–168.

Ministry of Education (1999) *Creating the Future Together: National Minimum Curriculum*. Malta: Ministry of Education.

Nieto, S. (1994) 'Lessons from the students on creating a chance to dream.' *Harvard Educational Review 64*, 4, 392–426.

Norwich, B. and Kelly, N.A.A. (2006) 'Evaluating children's participation in SEN procedures: Lessons for educational psychologists.' *Educational Psychology in Practice 22*, 3, 255–272.

Patterson, G.R., Reid, J.B. and Dishion, T. (1992) *Antisocial Boys: A Social Interactional Approach (Vol. 4)*. Eugene, OR: Castalia Publishing Company.

Pianta, R.C. (1999) *Enhancing Relationships between Children and Teachers*. Washington, DC: American Psychological Association.

Polat, F. and Farrel, P. (2002) What was it like for you? Former pupils' reflections on a residential school for pupils with emotional and behavioural difficulties. *Emotional and Behavioural Difficulties 7*, 2, 97–108.

Riley, K. (2004) 'Voices of disaffected pupils: Implications for policy and practice.' *British Journal of Educational Studies 52*, 2, 166–179.

Ruddock J. (2002) What's in it for us? Pupil consultation and participation. *The ESRC Network Project Newsletter No.4*. Available at www.consultingpupils.co.uk, accessed on 4 March 2009.

Ruddock, J. and Flutter, J. (2000) 'Pupil participation and pupil perspective: "carving a new order of experience."' *Cambridge Journal of Education 30*, 1, 75–86.

Smeets, E., Van der Veen, I., Derriks, M. and Roeleveld, J. (2007) *Zorgleerlingen en leerlingenzorg op de basisschool* [Pupils with special educational needs and special needs education in mainstream primary schools]. Nijmegen/Amsterdam: ITS/SCO-Kohnstamm Instituut.

Spera, C. and Wentzel, K.R. (2003) 'Congruence between students' and teachers' goals: Implications for social and academic motivation.' *International Journal of Educational Research 39*, 4–5, 395–413.

Spiteri, D. (2009) 'The Perspectives of Ex Students on Their Experiences at a School for Students with SEBD.' In C. Cefai and P. Cooper (eds) *Promoting Emotional Education: Connecting with Students in Difficulty*. London: Jessica Kingsley Publishers.

Toynbee, F. (1999) *'I've learned the value of people': Pupil perspectives of off-site education*. Unpublished MA dissertation. Institute of Education, University of London.

Wetton, N. and Williams, T. (2000) *Health for Life: Healthy Schools, Healthy Citizens*. Waltom-on-Thames: Nelson.

Whitty, G. and Wisby, E. (2007) *Real Decision Making: School Councils in Action*. Research Report DCSF-RR001. Department for Children, Schools and Families.

Wood, E. (2003) 'The power of pupil perspectives in evidence-based practice: The case of gender and underachievement.' *Research Papers in Education 18*, 4, 365–383.

World Health Organization (2008) *Inequalities in Young People's Health: School-Aged Children International Report From the 2005/2006 Survey*. Available at www.euro.who.int/Document/E91416.pdf, accessed 4 March 2009.

Young Minds (1999) *Spotlight* No.1. London: Young Minds.

CHAPTER 4

The Perspectives of Ex-Students on Their Experiences at a School for SEBD

Damian Spiteri

INTRODUCTION

There is a considerable debate in the literature about what type of educational provision is best suited to cater for the needs of young people considered at risk, particularly those with SEBD (Ofsted 2005). On one hand, students who are disruptive at school are seen as constituting the highest barrier to raising standards in schools (Lamb 2006), while it may be argued on the other that they may not derive benefits from ordinary schools since their behavior requires particularly skilful and vigilant management that is hard to come by in mainstream schools (Ofsted 1999). In this respect, having special schools could be seen as being consonant with the educational needs of the students, which may include needs arising from problems in learning, social interactions and mental health (Her Majesty's Inspectorate for Education and Training in Wales 2007).

Yet, in exploring what students are unable to do, such studies tend to subscribe to a 'deficit' understanding (Lipsky 1992) of the educational process and of students with SEBD themselves. Consequently, they fail to focus on the subjective meanings that the young people themselves ascribe to what they have achieved from their education. This chapter will go beyond such an approach and focus instead on analyzing how a cohort of young people who once attended an offsite special school developed self-efficacy, agency and resilience, and how their school experience empowered them to develop their own goals and reach them when they were older. This chapter presents the participants' own accounts of their educational experiences that they then used as 'strengths' as they moved into adulthood. It describes the various processes that served to influence their decisions both when at school and upon eventually leaving and starting their own lives as adults. Rather than focusing on this period as an isolated aspect or time-period of their lives, the author will thereby adopt a life-course approach (Hunt 2005) that is geared to exploring 'the total space' (Levy 1991, p.90) in which the lives of these people evolved.

THEORETICAL FRAMEWORK

Evidence-based studies are of empirical interest for a number of reasons. First, they are not only carried out in an empirical manner but are clearly seen to be so by virtue of the methodology selected and the transparency of the manner in which results are arrived at and presented (Concoran and Vandiver 2006). Second, evidence-based studies are usually interdisciplinary in focus and are therefore suited to a wide readership of professionals from different fields. Indeed, few issues are the purview of a single discipline (Thyer 2006). Findings from the educational field can easily be of interest to other professionals including counselors, play-therapists, nurses, psychiatrists, and many others. Conversely, educational researchers need to draw on interdisciplinary-derived research and be familiar with the findings and research practices of practitioners from other fields besides their own.

Evidence-based studies relating to students with SEBD are associated with finding out what works (Cooper 2001). One of the implications of this approach, is ensuring that any interventions that have been made in the participants' lives when they were children and adolescents were optimally effective at essential points of their life-course. Since the focus of this chapter is on student voices, which in itself is a research strategy 'that is relatively rare and scarce' (Nieto 1994, p.396), it thereby overrides the problem of defining which behaviors can be classed as symptomatic of SEBD, which can range from deep-seated emotional disturbances on one hand, to some form of reaction to outward circumstances on the other (DfEE 1994). In this manner, research has been carried out 'with' rather than 'on' the participants (Schulz 2000). Naturally, this subjective focus is also influenced by various factors related to the students' educational experience, such as the influence of the educators. Areas of knowledge overlap, and any evidence used must thus be integrated within the overlap between these different areas. Figure 4.1

provides an illustration of these overlapping spheres of influence. The interdisciplinary aspect of the model is clearly indicated, since best evidence cannot be derived by looking only at a single area of knowledge without considering the others. The same can be said for educators' knowledge and skills, wherein the delivery of lessons to students of varying academic abilities can be consolidated by relevant insights from different disciplines. The model also considers students' desires as part of this overall paradigm, thus serving to attribute due weighting to the student-centered focus of the evidence-based approach that is adopted in this chapter.

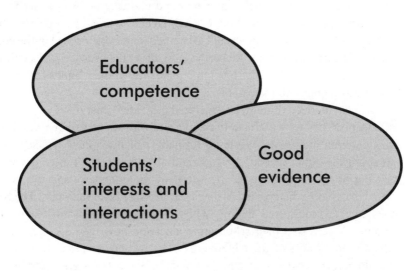

Figure 4.1: A model of evidence-based practice

METHODOLOGY

This chapter presents the finding of a small-scale, qualitative study that employs a grounded theory methodology in seeking to understand the students' educational experiences and its impact on their lives. It is based on data provided by a cohort of ex-students at St. Paul's School (not real name) who are presently in their mid-twenties and who attended the school during the school year 1995/1996. St. Paul's School is a second opportunity school in Malta for 14- to 16-year-old boys who have been identified as needing a special educational provision due to their disruptive behavior or to their unauthorized long-term absenteeism. The school has its own particular curriculum, with an emphasis on crafts and co-curricular and extra-curricular activities.

The total school population does not normally exceed 25 students. Students are usually sent to the school from state secondary schools catering for students with relatively low achievement levels.

The 12 participants in the study were a rather homogeneous group in terms of their socio-economic background, as they all came from low socio-economic status (SES) and eventually all came to be employed in one or more low SES jobs. Pierre worked at a bakery and also as a disc-jockey, Marc as an aluminium window fitter, Jean Paul as an attendant at a take-away establishment, Christopher as a laborer in a metal-forging establishment, Leroy as a bus-driver, Michel as a painter and plasterer, Louis as a mechanic, and Patrice as an electrician. Like Michel, Jacques worked as a painter and plasterer, Gilbert as a taxi-driver, and Olaf and Henri both worked in the construction industry as laborers. All participants, other than Patrice, had a wife or female partner and all lived with her independently of their families of origin. Patrice was living with his parents.

Data was derived through unstructured individual interviews with the 12 participants. They were each interviewed twice with an interval of around one week between interviews. While no formally structured interview schedule was applied in either session, the goals and objectives of each interview were spelt out to the participants at the outset of the interviews and they were invited to explore whatever issues they considered to be of relevance. The first interview was conducted mainly with the aim of establishing how the participants perceived their schooling overall and how they deemed this to influence any aspect of their life-course. The second interview focused on what the researcher designated as the common points that were raised by the participants in the first interview. In this way a core theory was developed from the data as presented by the participants. This approach was considered to give rise to a context where any arising narratives would emerge from a free-flowing 'dialogue' between the researcher and participant.

The interviews were aimed at promoting conversation and were based on Friere's (1992) concept of promoting 'horizontal relationships'. Such relationships allow for empathy to be generated between all those involved in the dialogue. This is furthermore conducive to any data collected being 'naturally occurring', in the sense that even had the observer not been present, it could be safely assumed that the resulting data would be the same (Griffin 2007).

Using a grounded theory approach, data is first grouped into categories and then into subcategories based on the categories as originally proposed (Glaser and Strauss 1967). The analysis is not something linear and usually involves further categories being introduced that stem from the subcategories as originally proposed. When all categories and subcategories have been delineated and when the data is seen to yield no more of them, then theoretical saturation is said to have been reached. At that stage, a core theory can be proposed (*ibid.*). Within the context of this study, the original categories developed included: personal autonomy in choosing what to learn at school; no preferential treatment by teachers amongst students; liaison with the home for psycho-social support; liaison with the home for material support; meaningful relationships with school staff; healthy peer support; and lack of bullying. These were then collapsed under three main headings that have been used to structure the analytical part of the study, namely, the Head of school's influence, the personalized attention provided to the students, and meaningful peer relationships.

MAJOR THEMES IN THE STUDY
The Head of school's influence

There is nothing novel about referring to a Head of school in the context of successful educational interventions, since this is something that can be traced to the beginning of effective schools research in the late 1960s (Kaplan and Usdan 1992). As time passed, however, it came to be increasingly recognized that an exclusive drive for academic excellence would have an overall negative effect on educational equity, and great consideration needed to be given to the diversity of students in the classroom if such equity was to be reached (Passow 1984). This particular dimension of equity as epitomized by the Head of school, was underlined by the participants:

> I did not want to learn the stuff they were trying to teach me at the secondary school that I used to go to. Who gave the right to the teachers to try to force me to learn things? At St. Paul's School, the headmaster told me 'over here you will learn what it is that you want to learn.' There were no extra-clever students. Everyone was the same. (Pierre)

Olaf and Patrice noted that at times the Head would visit them in their homes and even though they knew that this went over and beyond his call of duty, it helped them to feel significant as individuals:

> The thing that he used to come home to see us helped me – my eldest brother had a drug problem. He helped with that. He had also done everything he could so that the [negatively inclined] friends of my brother did not become my friends as well. ... If it was not for this, today, I would be hooked on drugs. (Olaf)

> The headmaster assisted my mother a lot to have a proper bathroom at her place. The headmaster had found some ex-students and that had showed me how to install and fix up a bathroom. If it was not for him, I would probably not even be working today, as I did not have any motivation to push me along. ... Today, I have a good job, the pay could be better, but the wage is steady and that is what is important to me. (Patrice)

Teaching and learning at St. Paul's went beyond traditional teaching. As a result of the interactive influence of their Head when they were younger, Olaf and Patrice eventually felt more empowered to achieve their goals. They observed that the Head's empowering approach and his out-of-school interventions enabled them to feel more confident and competent in mastering the challenges of life outside.

Personalized attention

The Head's interventions are highly interwoven with the second theme developed from the data, namely a school culture where students felt that they could work towards their aspirations successfully. Pierre had started off working as an employee in a shop where he served as a vendor of traditional Maltese snacks. He then saved up his earnings to establish himself in business as a part-time, self-employed, disc-jockey whilst working also at a bakery. He relates these achievements to his experiences at St. Paul's:

> At St. Paul's School, they were set on talking to you, on getting to know you. Even the thing that I used to play billiards with the teachers or with my friends helped me, because it was from there that I earned confidence. Then, there was this teacher whom we used to call the Englishman. He was never discouraged by anything and told me to help him embellish the school. Then, there was this social worker who was assigned to me by the school itself and who had come to see me both at school and at home on various occasions. When he once came home, he told me that 'you need to believe if you are to achieve'. I still remember those words. I carry them with me everywhere I go. ... It is because of this that today I can believe in myself enough to move on in business. Perhaps one day I will not need to be an employee anymore and will be totally self-employed as a DJ which is something I love. (Pierre)

Pierre's assertion about his being asked by a teacher to help him 'embellish' the school shows that the teachers' individual expertise and their use of the pedagogic knowledge is integrated with the students' values and expectations, through horizontal ways of relating (Friere 1992). Pierre's social worker who served as a bridge between the school and the home, served to instill in him a greater sense of safety and security when he was at the school.

Louis' story shows how being made to feel significant was related to the work he eventually took up when he left school. He explained that even though there was no course in automobile mechanics at the school, once the staff got to know of his wish to learn motor mechanics, they sought to help him develop this skill. The Head managed to procure a broken-down car, while another teacher helped him to dismantle it while explaining the function of each part. What Louis was hinting at was the manner in which St. Paul's, possibly unlike his previous mainstream school, was able to adopt a more student-centered approach due to the small number of students present and the particular school-management approach:

> For me, the most important thing is that teachers show you that they care about you and that they understand you. Today I am a mechanic. I have always wanted to be a mechanic. At school, I was allowed to dismantle and reassemble parts of a broken-down car. What more could I have possibly wanted then? The teachers there gave me the courage to say this is what I want to do, and I am going to do it. (Louis)

A further instance of individualized attention was mentioned by Michel who claimed that the Head had helped him to find his first job. He asserted that he knew someone who could employ him but did not know how to approach that person or what to say. The Head had engaged one of the teachers in fashioning out a role-play as to what was to be said over the telephone. Michel underlined that in future jobs, he had no problem in speaking to people and asking for jobs:

> I think the most important thing to me was leaving school and finding a job. It could have been any job. So long as it was a job. Looking back, I would say that it was the way that the teachers at St. Paul's School treated me that helped me along. For instance, if I had to pick up a fight, I would have done so very easily. Yet, if it came to asking someone for a job, I simply did not know how to do it. The teachers helped me to become more confident. They showed me how to 'act' confident. That is all I needed then. Today, because of what they taught me, I would say that I am not only confident but mega-confident. (Michel)

Teaching was thereby geared toward identifying ways in which the teachers and other staff succeeded in improving the students' social skills and interpersonal problem-solving ability. By listening to them and by understanding and reflecting on their feelings and individual motivation, they empowered the participants to 'understand, process, manage, and express the social and emotional aspects of [their] lives' (Cohen 2001, p.3); eventually this helped them to find purpose in their lives later on as adults.

Meaningful peer relationships

Peer-relationships are another aspect of schooling that was considered to have had an impact on the adult lives of the participants. Henri notes that in the mainstream secondary school that he attended prior to St. Paul's, it was common for young people from a one particular locality to bully and harass those from another locality. He claimed that this did not happen at St. Paul's, and had he not been transferred there, he would have suffered a great deal:

> I do not know why I was always seen as the trouble-maker. I am actually a quiet person. I just want to be left in peace. This was the way I was at school and I am still that way today. I think that at St. Paul's what the teachers taught me was to identify people who were too difficult for me to handle and to avoid them. Even though (in my adult life) I once worked at a job where I was bullied, I remembered what the teachers had told me that once you walk into a situation, then if you find out that it is too much for you, then you must walk out, and walk on. That is what I did and have always done since then. (Henri)

The way in which Henri describes himself does not portray such characteristics that are usually associated with SEBD, such as being disruptive or engaging in delinquent behavior. Nonetheless, he appears to have been disaffected with his school and this seems to have been found to be challenging by his mainstream teachers. At St. Paul's, he deems as significant that he learnt to choose the people whom he felt he could trust. St. Paul's is thereby not placed amongst the schools promoting masculinized school subcultures that are often seen as contributing to the development of poor attitudes and lack of motivation amongst boys (see Jackson 1998; Willis 1977). There is no emphasis on the need for Henri to be tough, to act out, to be cool, or to be one of the lads. Rather, there is an emphasis on interpersonal skills and on developing one's individual strengths in engaging in prosocial peer interactions.

Peer relationships were also instrumental in the life of Gilbert. Gilbert claimed that he had been picked on in his previous mainstream school and was often described as being 'effeminate'. Moreover, he had no interest in matters that seemed to interest his peers, and for this reason he often felt the odd one out. He claimed that:

> Over there [at the mainstream school], they used to call me names time and time over. Because of what they told me, I went through a crisis.

I wanted to be liked by my friends. Yet, they kept on calling me girlish. Then at St. Paul's School, I found these teachers who played billiards with the students and told the students to include me in the games. From then on, I made friends. Nobody insulted me anymore. I started to go out with peers. Previous to that, I have never been out with friends before. Today, I would say that St. Paul's School gave me confidence. I work as a taxi-driver, and I work with all sorts of people. I would say that making friends at school and then going out were where it all started from. (Gilbert)

Judging by the way Henri and Gilbert described St. Paul's, the school appeared to subscribe to Sukhnandan's (2000, p.15) idea that it created 'a culture where male students can achieve without fear of ridicule and where disruptive behavior is not allowed to undermine learning'. In Henri's case, this particular type of school culture 'can assist students to challenge the social construction of gendered behaviors' by engaging them in being themselves rather than promoting stereotypical behaviors, such as having to prove one's masculinity by being tough or by fighting back. In Gilbert's case, it underlines that students with SEBD are particularly vulnerable to social-emotional problems and social-skills deficits. This is related to the definition of SEBD in young people as one where the behaviors and emotions that these young people manifest are what is essentially the manner of concern (Visser 2003).

CONCLUSION

The core concept that links the above themes together is that people matter. It is clear from their narratives that, as students, the participants had no interest in finding out if they were labeled individually or collectively as students with SEBD. Rather, they wanted to be given positive strokes by having their strengths and positive qualities acknowledged through their schooling. The theoretical model that is proposed in this chapter suggests that evidence-based interventions cannot simply be based on educators' expertise, best evidence, or students' desires, without taking into consideration the interrelationships between these factors. This can be particularly seen through the students presenting an 'I want to be involved' discourse. They were seeking to have functional relationships with their teachers and anticipated that this would be reciprocal. The skills that they employed in building relationships of this nature are what they would then re-employ in different contexts throughout their life-course.

Even though the study was limited by its being a study of young men only, it shows how people can be socialized to develop a critical social intelligence and self-reflexivity about how they engage in particular social behaviors. Moreover, despite the small number of participants selected, the study was intended to offer an in-depth appraisal of significant events that the participants could trace back as having been positively influenced by their experience at St. Paul's. It is hoped that it will pave the way for further studies on how students with SEBD cope when they attend mainstream schools. This could then lead to differential studies on the needs of boys and girls who present SEBD in both mainstream and special provision.

The participants reported that their attendance at St. Paul's School had a positive effect on the manner in which their life-course developed as young adult workers. Importance was attributed to the interventions of the Head of school, the school's attention to links with the students' home and community, and to a student-centered school culture that enabled students to feel that they were individuals rather than 'one of a number'. All in all, this made them feel that their participation at school was valued and consequently gave them strength and belief in themselves in the social contexts they encountered once they finished school and started their journey into adulthood.

REFERENCES

Cohen, J. (ed.) (2001) *Caring Classrooms/Intelligent Schools: The Social Emotional Education of Young Children.* New York: Teachers College Press.

Concoran, K. and Vandiver, V.L. (2006) 'Implementing Best Practice and Expert Consensus Procedures.' In A.R. Roberts and K.R. Yeager (eds) *Foundations of Evidence-Based Social Work Practice* (pp.59–66). Oxford: Oxford University Press.

Cooper, P. (2001) *We Can Work It Out: What Works in Education for Pupils with Social, Emotional and Behavioural Difficulties Outside Mainstream Classrooms?* Ilford: Barnardo's.

Department for Education and Employment (DFEE) (1994) *The Education of Children with Emotional and Behavioural Difficulties.* Circular 9/94. Nottingham: DfEE Publications.

Her Majesty's Inspectorate for Education and Training in Wales (2007) *Evaluating Outcomes for Children and Young People with Additional Learning Needs.* Cardiff: Estyn.

Friere, P. (1992) *Education for Critical Consciousness.* New York: Continuum.

Glaser, B.G. and Strauss, A.M. (1967) *The Discovery of Grounded Theory: Strategies for Qualitative Research.* New York: Aldine.

Griffin, C. (2007) 'Being dead and being there: Research interviews, sharing hand cream and the preference for analysing "naturally occurring data".' *Discourse Studies 9*, 246–269.

Hunt, S. (2005) *The Life Course: A Sociological Introduction.* New York: Palgrave Macmillan.

Jackson, D. (1998) 'Breaking out of the Binary Trap: Boys' Underachievement, Schooling and Gender Relations.' In D. Epstein, J. Elwood, V. Hey and J. Maw (eds) *Failing Boys?* Buckingham: Open University Press.

Kaplan, G. and Usdan, M. (1992) 'The changing look of education's policy networks.' Phi Delta Kappa 73, 9, 664–672.

Lamb, T. (2006) 'Reconceptualizing Disaffection: Issues of Power, Voice and Learner Autonomy.' In C. Borg and C. Calleja (eds) *Understanding Children and Youth At Risk: Narratives of Hope* (pp.1–30). Malta: Media Centre Publications.

Levy, R. (1991) 'Status Passages as Critical Life-course Transitions.' In W.R. Heinz (ed.) *Theoretical Advances in Life-course Research* (pp.87–114). Weinheim: Deutscher Studien Verlag.

Lipsky, D.K. (1992) 'Achieving Full Inclusion: Placing the Students at the Center of Educational Reform.' In W. Stainback and S. Stainback (eds) *Controversial Issues Confronting Special Education: Divergent Perspectives.* Boston, MA: Allyn and Bacon.

Nieto, S. (1994) 'Lessons from the students on creating a chance to dream.' *Harvard Educational Review 64*, 4, 392–426.

Office for Standards in Education (Ofsted) (1999) *Principles into Practice: Effective Education for Pupils with EBD.* HMI report. London: Ofsted.

Office for Standards in Education (Ofsted) (2005) *Managing Challenging Behaviour.* London. Ofsted.

Passow, A. (1984) 'Tackling the reform reports of the 1980s.' *Phi Delta Kappa 65*, 10, 674–683.

Schulz, R. (2000) 'Collaborative Narrative Inquiry and the Ethic of Caring.' In W.E. Schutz (ed.) *Counselling Ethics Case Book, 2000* (2nd edition) (pp.212–218). Ottawa: Canadian Counselling Association.

Sukhnandan, L. (2000) *An Investigation into Gender Differences in Achievement: Phase 1: A Review of Recent Research and LEA Information on Provision.* London: National Foundation for Educational Research.

Thyer, B. (2006) 'What is Evidenced-Based Practice?' In A.R. Roberts and K.R. Yeager (eds) *Foundations of Evidence-Based Social Work Practice.* pp.35–46). Oxford: Oxford University Press.

Visser, J. (2003) *A Study of Young People with Challenging Behaviour.* London: Ofsted.

Willis, P. (1977) *Learning to Labour.* Farnborough: Saxon House.

CHAPTER 5

The Perspectives of Students on Personal and Social Development in School

Mark G. Borg and Andrew Triganza Scott

INTRODUCTION

The mission statement as set out in the Personal and Social Development (PSD) Curriculum in Malta (Ministry of Education, Youth and Employment 2005a, 2005b, p.3) declares that:

> PSD aims at empowering individuals to develop skills that enhance their wellbeing, by identifying and developing their potential, thus enabling them to participate effectively in their social environment.

This initiative was meant 'to reflect the physical, social, cognitive, moral and psychological needs of the students' (Abela *et al.* 2001).

About 20 years after PSD was first introduced as a curricular subject in Maltese schools (albeit under different names, labels, forms and formats) it is not impertinent to ask: 'To what extent is this "mission" being achieved?' Indeed, one may even wish to probe further and ask: 'To what extent are the aims set out for each grade level being achieved?' (Ministry of Education, Youth and Employment 2005a, 2005b). 'How is it impacting on the students?' 'Is it merely informative or is it serving its formative role?' Although there have been a number of small-scale studies which have tried to fathom the attitudes of students towards PSD (e.g. Bonello 2003; Dalmas 1997), and an attempt at the PSD curriculum evaluation (Muscat 2006), there is very little empirical evidence of the impact that PSD is having on successive student cohorts. In this absence one may to turn to circumstantial, 'second-best', indirect evidence, which may nevertheless be useful in unravelling the situation. For instance, the general impressions among education personnel and parents include:

- PSD is very popular among students
- it is an interesting and enjoyable subject
- it serves informative and formative roles
- generally, it impacts positively on most students, empowering them and helping them to develop a number personal and social attitudes and skills.

REVIEW OF THE LITERATURE

This review is organized in two sections. The first tries to outline the historical background to the development of PSD as a programme in Maltese schools. The second will review the one substantial empirical study evaluating this initiative carried in Malta so far.

Historical background

PSD in Maltese schools knows its roots as 'life skills' in Church schools, where it was introduced in the mid 1980s as a timetabled curricular subject (Sultana 1992). Its name evolved to 'personal and social skills' (Muscat 2006) and then, with its inclusion in the National Minimum Curriculum at the Secondary Level (Ministry of Education 1990) and its subsequent introduction as a formal curriculum subject in Grades 7 and 8 (11 and 12-year-olds) of state secondary schools in 1989, to 'personal and social education' (PSE). Following the National Minimum Curriculum of 1999 (Ministry of Education 1999) it was introduced also in some state primary schools where there were acute behavioural problems. It was at about this time that its name was changed to its current form: 'personal and social development' (PSD), lifted from the National Guidelines of the Scottish Office Education Department (June 1993) (see Giordmaina 2000, p.192). In 2002 a proposal for a PSD syllabus for primary and secondary schools (Abela Cefai *et al.* 2002) was commissioned by and submitted to the National Curriculum Council (NCC), as part of the work of a focus group set up to advise the NCC. This document was effectively adopted in its original form by the Education Division (Ministry of Education,

Youth and Employment 2005a, 2005b), taking on only a token recommendation of the very valid ones proposed by Sultana and Fenech (2003) in an evaluation of the document on behalf of the NCC. In the following few years it was eventually introduced in all primary schools and in all grade levels. The year 2007 saw the Maltese education authorities restricting PSD in state schools to the last three years of the primary cycle.

Apart from introducing a series of topics believed to be of immediate relevance to the personal and social needs of students across the compulsory school years and possibly even beyond, PSD, which is as much a question of method as of content (White, as cited in Sultana 1992), was meant to break the mould of teaching at examinations, of pure traditional instruction, of an education that is irrelevant to the needs of the students, of separating out the students who can from those who can't. This, together with a methodology that emphasizes experiential learning, a pedagogy that is student-centred, and an organization that sees student groups of not more than 15 at a time, were meant 'to humanise institutions and motivate students' (Sultana 1992, p.169). Of the latter, there are those whom the system had 'failed' in more than one sense of the word. 'Failed' them because they had been labelled 'failures' and 'hopeless' earlier on in their scholastic career and treated as such ever since. 'Failed' them because the education system has been irrelevant to their immediate and future needs and aspirations. Central in all this is the shift in role of the teacher from that of an instructor to that of a facilitator and role model; the PSD facilitator becomes the teacher and the learner at one and the same time (Muscat 2006).

It does not fall within the purposes of the present chapter to delve critically into the relevance, educational and sociological impact of the content of the PSD syllabus and its implications (e.g. see Sultana 1992; Sultana and Fenech 2003). Suffice it to outline these topics, not least to appreciate and understand better the responses of the surveyed students. Fig 5.1 sets out a schematic outline of the PSD 'topics' covered throughout the compulsory school years in state schools (Ministry of Education, Youth and Employment 2005a, 2005b).

Evaluation of the PSD initiative

As pointed out above, there has only been one notable study evaluating PSD in Maltese schools, namely that carried out by Muscat (2006). Employing a mixed methodology approach, 407 boys and girls in Grade 7, 8 and 9 (ages 11, 12, 13-year-olds) from state and Church secondary schools completed a

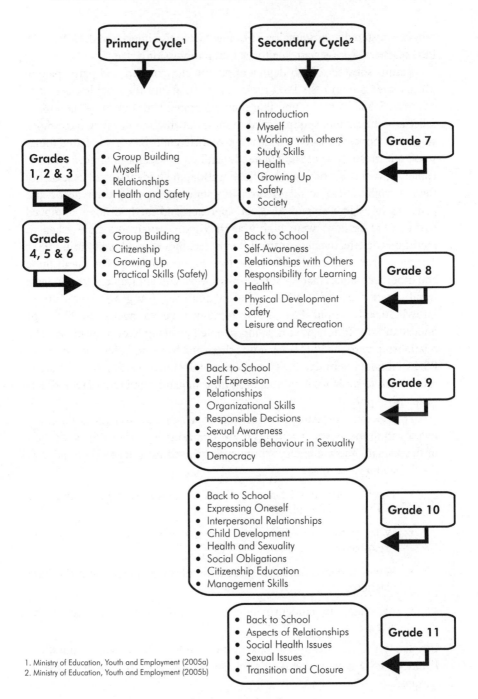

Primary Cycle[1]

Secondary Cycle[2]

Grades 1, 2 & 3
- Group Building
- Myself
- Relationships
- Health and Safety

Grade 7
- Introduction
- Myself
- Working with others
- Study Skills
- Health
- Growing Up
- Safety
- Society

Grades 4, 5 & 6
- Group Building
- Citizenship
- Growing Up
- Practical Skills (Safety)

Grade 8
- Back to School
- Self-Awareness
- Relationships with Others
- Responsibility for Learning
- Health
- Physical Development
- Safety
- Leisure and Recreation

Grade 9
- Back to School
- Self Expression
- Relationships
- Organizational Skills
- Responsible Decisions
- Sexual Awareness
- Responsible Behaviour in Sexuality
- Democracy

Grade 10
- Back to School
- Expressing Oneself
- Interpersonal Relationships
- Child Development
- Health and Sexuality
- Social Obligations
- Citizenship Education
- Management Skills

Grade 11
- Back to School
- Aspects of Relationships
- Social Health Issues
- Sexual Issues
- Transition and Closure

1. Ministry of Education, Youth and Employment (2005a)
2. Ministry of Education, Youth and Employment (2005b)

Figure 5.1: The current PSD syllabus – Outline by topic

self-administered questionnaire; 36 of these were also interviewed. Of their 11 PSD teachers, 8 took part in a focus group discussion.

Results showed a high degree of enjoyment, comfort and participation. Most students found the PSD topics very useful and the teaching activities effective. Students also found that they integrated better in the PSD setting, especially the smaller group. Asked to indicate which topics they liked most, student responses revealed a wide range of different topics. Two related topics stood out irrespective of student gender and school sector in Grades 7 and 8, namely sexual education and health education; in Grade 9, issues in sexuality figured high. These were perceived by students to meet their needs and concerns to a large extent. Also, the approach and methodology employed during PSD sessions were highly appreciated. Participants were asked to report on the effectiveness of the different techniques employed during PSD. The most 'useful' were discussions, videos and group work. The use of these and other techniques made PSD sessions special and enjoyable. Also, students rated seven out of eight facilitator qualities (ranging from 'Being knowledgeable about PSD/PSD' to 'Sensitive to needs' to 'Easy to understand' to 'In touch with young people') as being 'Good' or better. The relationship with the PSD teacher was cherished by most. Indeed, not only are PSD facilitators central to the effectiveness of the initiative, but they also act as role models to students. A number of significant gender and school type effects were also reported.

This chapter presents the findings of a subsequent large-scale study investigating the views of students towards various aspects of PSD at the end of the primary and secondary school cycles. Specifically, it sought to address the following questions:

- How popular is PSD among Grade 6 (11-year-olds) and Grade 11 (16-year-olds) students?

- What is their opinion of the topics covered and how they were organized?

- What is their opinion of the methodology employed and the PSD teacher?

- Are there any student gender and school sector differences in the above?

Ultimately, the aim was to provide empirical evidence to answer the question: If indeed PSD is very popular, is this so for the 'right' or for the 'wrong' reasons?

METHODOLOGY
Participants

Two target samples, each of 1000 schoolchildren, were selected to represent the population in terms of school sector and gender balance. Pupils in the primary school sample were drawn from Grade 6 (age 11), while those in the secondary school sample were from Grade 11 (age 16). Eventually, a total of 1750 Maltese schoolchildren participated in the survey by completing a self-administered questionnaire. This represents a response rate of 85 per cent and 90 per cent for the two samples. As is evident from Table 5.1, the resulting samples consisted of equal numbers of boys and girls across grade level and school sector. The proportions of students drawn from each sector roughly approximates to the proportions for the whole population.

Table 5.1: Student samples by gender and school sector			
	Boys	**Girls**	**Total**
Grade 6	425 (50%)	425 (50%)	850 (100%)
Grade 11	450 (50%)	450 (50%)	900 (100%)
Grade 6			
Independent schools	49 (49%)	51 (51%)	100 (100%)
Church schools	76 (51%)	74 (49%)	150 (100%)
State schools	300 (50%)	300 (50%)	600 (100%)
Grade 11			
Independent schools	50 (50%)	50 (50%)	100 (100%)
Church schools	100 (50%)	100 (50%)	200 (100%)
State schools	300 (50%)	300 (50%)	600 (100%)

The questionnaires

Two anonymous, self-administered questionnaires were developed. A focus group with six PSD teachers from the various sectors was held to identify key issues. The first version of the two questionnaires was submitted to the same group of teachers for their feedback. Following a number of modifications the pilot version of the two questionnaires was formulated and administered on a small group of schoolchildren from the two grade levels.

The Grade 6 questionnaire consisted of three sections. The first section requested information about the respondents' gender and school sector attended. The second section consisted of eight statements (plus an inverted one) about the PSD session, topics, methodology and teacher, which the respondents had to rate on a three-point scale. In the third section the respondent was requested to indicate whether they like or dislike PSD and the reasons why; the three topics they liked best; and the three topics they disliked most.

The Grade 11 questionnaire consisted of two sections. The first section requested information about the respondents' gender, school sector attended, and when they started having PSD lessons (i.e. at the primary or the secondary level). The second section consisted of six questions. The first two requested respondents to indicate whether they like PSD and the reasons why; and whether they enjoy their PSD lessons and the reasons why. The next two questions sought to unravel the three most interesting, and the three least interesting, topics. The last two questions asked respondents to indicate whether there are topics they would like to see (a) dropped, and, if so, which ones; and (b) included, and, if so, which ones.

FINDINGS AND DISCUSSION

This section is organized in two sub-sections; the first will consider the major findings from the Grade 6 survey, while the second will focus on the Grade 11 survey. (Data were analysed using the SPSS15 statistical software package. Gender and school sector effects were investigated employing the chi-square test of independence.)

Grade 6

Table 5.2 [a] sets out in rank order the Grade 6 students' 'happy' reactions to the eight statements about the PSD session, topics, methodology and teacher. About 93 per cent expressed 'happiness' when it is time for the PSD lesson and with the prospect of more such lessons. The actual PSD lesson and the PSD teacher continue to contribute to the high 'approval rating' for the subject. It is perhaps significant that students are progressively less approving as statements start covering actual PSD activities, with working on PSD copybook obtaining 50 per cent approval.

The investigation of gender and school sector effects yielded two important findings. The first, that significantly more girls expressed 'happy' reactions than boys in five of the eight statements. This suggests that by the end of the primary cycle, girls are more satisfied with specific aspects of PSD than the boys. The second finding was that there are no school sector effects, suggesting that students across the three school sectors are happy with the various aspects of PSD to the same degree.

Table 5.2: Grade 6 students' 'Happy' reactions* to PSD effects	
[a] in rank order	
When it is time for PSD lessons	92.9%
More PSD lessons	92.7%
During PSD lessons	83.6%
As the PSD teacher enters class	82.2%
The topics covered in PSD	78.1%
Discussions during PSD	75.8%
When asked to speak during PSD	60.5%
Working on PSD copybooks	50.4%
[b] gender effects	**Proportionally more**
Working on PSD copybooks	Girls
Discussions during PSD	Girls
The topics covered in PSD	Girls
During PSD lessons	Girls
When it is time for PSD lessons	Girls

*Abridged statements

Table 5.3: Grade 6 students' reasons* for liking PSD	
Helps me understand others	93.1%
Lessons are very interesting	93.0%
We have time to discuss things	92.0%
I can share what I think	92.0%
It is a load of fun	91.2%
We have time to stop and think	83.6%
I like the PSD teacher	77.9%
There are no tests and exams	65.7%
Organized in a smaller group	62.0%
There is no homework	52.9%

*Abridged statements

In answer to the question 'Do you like PSD?' almost all (98.5%) of the Grade 6 students answered 'Yes'. An investigation of the reasons behind this popularity reveals that the top five, each drawing more than 90 per cent of the sample, have to do with the impact that the subject has on students (*Helps me understand others*), the effects of the methodology employed (*We have time to discuss things; I can share what I think*), and conduct of PSD lessons (*Lessons are very interesting; It is a load of fun*) (Table 5.3). In view of the finding that the least popular reason for liking PSD is the lack of homework, one may conclude that PSD is much popular for the 'right' reasons.

Of the 13 respondents who indicated that they did not like PSD, seven indicated *More important things to do* and *Do not like expressing what I think*, while six indicated *I do not learn anything new* as the main reasons for their dislike.

Further analyses looked into the effects of gender and school sector. Again, we found no significant school sector effects; but significantly more boys than girls indicated lack of homework, tests and exams, and the small group organization of the lesson, as the reasons why they like PSD. Notably, two of these three reasons as indicated by the boys can be considered 'wrong' reasons for liking the subject. Then again, this (and the previous finding) may well reflect an indictment of the widespread exaggerated use of homework, tests and exams; a yearning for schooling practices that are less centered round these aspects.

Table 5.4: Grade 6 students' 'PSD topics I like best' *	
I can be assertive and make good decisions	65.1%
I get along well with friends and others	49.6%
I can protect myself from adults and decide which adults I can trust	46.5%
I can listen to others and express myself clearly	45.3%
We can help each other and how we can ask others for their help	41.3%
I take care of our environment – that of the school, the village and the country	36.7%
I organize my time and how to study	34.9%
We grow up and change in how we look	31.9%

*Abridged statements

Students were requested to indicate the PSD topics they liked best. By far, the most popular topic is *I can be assertive and make good decisions*, indicated by 65 per cent of the sample (see Table 5.4). This is followed by *I get along well with friends and others*, the preference of about 50 per cent of the students. It is perhaps not a coincidence that the two most popular topics have to do with personal and interpersonal skills. Furthermore, in view of the sample's age it should not be surprising that the least cited topic is *We grow up and change in how we look*.

A number of significant gender and school sector effects were evident. There were proportionally more boys than girls who liked topics dealing with taking care of the environment, how to help others and seek help, and how to listen to others and express oneself clearly; all of which have a social dimension. On the other hand, the topic *We grow up and change in how we look* is more liked by girls. While this topic figured as the least liked topic overall, it should not be surprising that it turned out to be more popular among the girls, even at this age.

The analysis of school sector effects revealed very few significant effects, indicating that role of school sector in the popularity of PSD topics is minimal. In the topics where there is an effect (*We grow up and change in how we look* and *I take care of the environment*), more students from Church schools liked these topics than those from the state and independent school sectors. This may well reflect the emphasis that PSD teachers in the Church school sector give to these topics. It may also reflect particular enthusiasm and commitment from teachers in this sector.

The responses of the 270 Grade 6 students who responded to the question about 'PSD topics I do NOT like the most' are set out in Table 5.5. Results show that the two least liked topics are *We grow up and change in how we look* and *I organize my time and how to study*, both indicated by about 41 per cent of the students. The topic that is least disliked is *I can be assertive and make good decisions*. In a sense, these findings corroborate those in Table 5.4, in that the most liked in one table appears as the least 'not liked' in the other and *vice versa*.

Table 5.5: Grade 6 students' 'PSD topics I do NOT like the most'*	
We grow up and change in how we look	41.3%
I organize my time and how to study	40.9%
I can protect myself from adults and decide which adults I can trust	32.7%
I take care of our environment – that of the school, the village and the country	32.7%
I can listen to others and express myself clearly	29.0%
I get along well with friends and others	25.3%
We can help each other and how we can ask others for their help	23.8%
I can be assertive and make good decisions	14.8%

*Abridged statements

The analysis of gender effects indicated no significant results except for the topic *I can listen to others and express myself clearly* with proportionally more boys citing it. That is, all of the topics but one were approximately disliked by both boys and girls in the subsample.

Similarly, with the exception of two topics there were no significant school sector effects. In the topics where there was an effect (*I can listen to others and express myself clearly* and *I take care of the environment*), more students from independent schools did not like these topics than those from the state and Church schools. The latter finding is the converse of the school sector in relation to liked topics, effect which therefore corroborate each other.

Grade 11

Almost 95 per cent of Grade 11 students declared that they liked PSD. The analyses investigating gender and school sector effects showed that whereas the subject is popular among both genders to more or less the same extent, significantly more students in state schools like PSD than those in independent and Church schools. It may well be that this 'lower' popularity of the subject among students from the non-state school sector can be explained by a perhaps more coherent methodology, proper set-up, and better resources in the state school sector.

Table 5.6 Reasons* given by Grade 11 students who like PSD	
6.2 [a] Reasons in rank order (n=854)	
It deals with interesting topics	73.5%
It prepares me for life	71.1%
It helps me understand myself better	61.9%
It is informative	59.6%
There are no tests and exams	58.4%
It deals with topics important to me	56.3%
It helps me understand others	47.5%
There is no homework	40.2%

*Abridged statements

The two top reasons for PSD popularity (Table 5.6) are *It deals with interesting topics* and *It prepares me for life*, both indicated by more than 71 per cent of those who like PSD. *There is no homework* ranked the least popular reason (40 per cent of the students). This is in line with the findings from the Grade 6 study. The subject most popular with Grade 11 students for the 'right' reasons (the content and conduct of lessons, and self-growth) and least popular for what may be considered a 'wrong' reasons. Further analyses indicated that more boys than girls cited the following reasons: *There is no homework* and *It helps me understand others.* This finding is in line with that reported for Grade 6 students.

The analyses of school sector effects revealed four significant results. There were significantly more Grade 11 students from independent schools who cited lack of homework than those from the Church and state school sectors. Moreover, students from the state school sector cited *It deals with topics important to me, It helps me understand myself better,* and *It prepares me for life* significantly more often than students from the Church and independent school sectors. It is perhaps significant that Grade 11 students in Church schools should emphasize most these formative aspects of the subject.

Respondents were also requested to indicate any other reason they felt was important. Of the 81 students who answered this open-ended question, 21 per cent indicated the opportunity to express oneself/debate/share ideas, 19 per cent indicated that PSD is relaxing, 12 per cent indicated teacher-related reasons, 7 per cent indicated that PSD is fun, and 5 per cent indicated understanding self and others.

Table 5.7 sets out in rank order the reasons cited by those 46 students who indicated that they did not like PSD. The two most 'popular' reasons are: *It is a waste of time* (75%) and *There are more important things to do* (just over 59%). It is clear that PSD's relevance and usefulness are not appreciated by these students. For less than a handful of students, lack of homework, repetition of lessons and too much probing during lessons, were other reasons for not liking the subject.

Table 5.7: Reasons* given by Grade 11 students who do NOT like PSD	
It is a waste of time	75.0%
There are more important things to do	59.1%
It does not really prepare me for life	34.1%
It does not deal with topics that are important to me	29.5%
It deals with embarrassing topics	25.0%
It is not informative enough	18.2%
There are no tests and exams	9.1%
There is no homework	6.8%

*Abridged statements

Grade 11 students were also asked to report whether they actually enjoyed PSD lessons and their reasons, and 94 per cent responded that they did. While this cuts across the two gender groups, significantly more students in state schools enjoy the subject than those in Church and independent schools.

The three top reasons indicated by the 846 students who enjoyed PSD (Table 5.8) were: *Lessons are in a small group, We students can discuss issues among ourselves,* and *I can express my thoughts and feelings openly.* It is perhaps significant that these have to do with how sessions are organized and the opportunity to express oneself through debates.

Table 5.8: Reasons* given by Grade 11 students who enjoy PSD lessons	
Lessons are in a small group	78.4%
We students can discuss issues among ourselves	64.9%
I can express my thoughts and feelings openly	64.4%
I learn new skills	54.7%
It has helped me to strengthen my relationships with friends	49.4%
We students take an active part	47.8%
My views are respected by the PSD teacher	45.4%
I like the PSD teacher	42.5%
I become aware of skills and work on them	42.5%
It is a load of fun	37.6%
I feel that my views are respected by fellow students	31.3%

*Abridged statements

An investigation of gender effects on the reasons for enjoying PSD showed that there were significantly more boys who indicated *I like the PSD teacher, My views are respected by the PSD teacher,* and *We students take an active part.* On the other hand, there were more girls who cited *It has helped me to strengthen my relationships with friends.*

With regard to school sector effects, that there were significantly more Grade 11 students in state schools than in the other two sectors who indicated the following reasons for enjoying the subject: *It is a load of fun, I like the PSD teacher, It has helped me to strengthen my relationships with friends* and *I learn new skills.* There were more students from independent schools who indicated *Lessons are in a small group,* and more from Church schools who cited *I become aware of skills and work on them* than students from the remaining two sectors.

Table 5.9 sets out the reasons for not enjoying PSD lessons as indicated by 54 students. The two most cited reasons are: *It is boring – I have learned nothing new* and *I do not learn any new skill.*

Table 5.9: Reasons* given by Grade 11 students who do not enjoy PSD lessons	
It is boring – I have learned nothing new	63.0%
I do not learn any new skill	50.0%
I do not like the PSD teacher	42.6%
It does not really help me to strengthen my relationships with friends	35.2%
I am not confident expressing my thoughts and feelings openly	33.3%
I feel that my views are not respected by fellow students	20.4%
I do not like being the centre of attention	20.4%
I feel embarrassed discussing certain topics	14.8%
My views are not respected by the PSD teacher	13.0%
Lessons are in a small group	13.0%
New skills are introduced but we do not work on them	11.1%

*Abridged statements

Asked to indicate which three topics they found most interesting, the Grade 11 sample indicated: *sex education, drug awareness,* and *relationships.* In a sense, the former and the latter were expected, these being adolescent students. On the other hand, the three least interesting were: *self-development and self-management, citizenship education,* and *drug awareness.* It is clear that *drug awareness* splits the sample in two – those who found it amongst the most interesting and those who find it amongst the least interesting. It may well be that over-exposing some of the students to the dangers of drug abuse may be 'boring' these students.

CONCLUSIONS

On the basis of the above findings it is clear that at the end of the primary and secondary cycles, PSD is overwhelmingly popular among students in Maltese state schools. This is very much in line with the findings reported by Muscat (2006). Grade 6 students indicated that it is an interesting, fun subject that allows discussion, thinking, the sharing of ideas and that helps them under-stand others. For Grade 11 students, the major reason for its popularity is that it treats interesting topics and prepares them for life. Notably, these include both informative and formative reasons. Moreover, among students in the two age groups, lack of homework figured as the least cited reason for liking the subject, while the absence of tests and exams figures among the least popular reasons. This, together with other findings, strongly suggests that PSD is popular and enjoyed for the 'right' reasons. Assertiveness and decision-making figure as the two most popular topics in the two age groups, with sex education topping the list among the older cohort.

Hence, one may conclude that PSD is overwhelming popular irrespective of gender and school sector, and it is predominantly so for the 'right' reasons. Nevertheless, there is a need to update the topics and consolidate the methodology and pedagogy so that the subject is strengthened across school types and sectors.

On the basis of what students themselves have reported, we may argue that the PSD experiences are indeed facilitating improved personal and interpersonal skills and general wellbeing in children and young persons. In so doing, PSD must to some extent be instrumental in promoting social, emotional and behavioural competence, if not preventing difficulties altogether. For this and this alone, it should – indeed must – be strengthened and consolidated.

REFERENCES

Abela, G., Azzopardi, A., Camilleri, K., Ciantar, M.A., Vancell, J. and Zammit Pulo, S. (2001) *Developmental Programme for PSD Teachers.* Unpublished manuscript, Malta.

Abela Cefai, G., Camilleri, K., Vancell, J. and Zammit Pulo, S. (2002) *PSD Syllabus 2002.* Malta: National Curriculum Council.

Bonello, C. (2003) *Attitudes Towards PSD Among Form Two Students.* Unpublished BEd (Hons) dissertation submitted to the Faculty of Education, University of Malta.

Dalmas, V.M. (1997) *Teachers' and Students' Attitudes Towards Personal and Social Education.* Unpublished BEd (Hons) dissertation submitted to the Faculty of Education, University of Malta.

Giordmaina, J. (ed.) (2000) *National Curriculum on Its Way: Proceedings of a Conference on the Implementation of the National Curriculum.* Ministry of Education/Division of Education/University of Malta, Malta.

Ministry of Education (1990) *National Minimum Curriculum for the Secondary Level.* Legal Notice 109 of 1990. Malta: Ministry of Education.

Ministry of Education (1999) *Creating the Future Together: National Minimum Curriculum.* Malta: Ministry of Education.

Ministry of Education, Youth and Employment (2005a) *Personal and Social Development: Syllabus for Primary Schools.* PSD Section, Department of Curriculum Management, Education Division, Malta.

Ministry of Education, Youth and Employment (2005b) *Personal and Social Development: Syllabus for Secondary Schools.* PSD Section, Department of Curriculum Management, Education Division, Malta.

Muscat, M. (2006) *An Evaluation of the Personal and Social Development Programme.* Unpublished MEd (Hons) dissertation submitted to the Faculty of Education, University of Malta.

Sultana, R.G. (1992) Personal and social education: Curriculum innovation and school bureaucracies in Malta. *British Journal of Guidance and Counselling 20,* 2, 164–185.

Sultana, R.G. and Fenech, J. (2003) *PSD Syllabus 2002: Evaluation Report.* Unpublished manuscript. Malta: National Curriculum Council.

PART 2

Mobilising Peer Support

CHAPTER 6

Peer Support Challenges School Bullying

Helen Cowie

INTRODUCTION

One of the commonest issues that children and young people raise as a factor that makes them unhappy at school concerns their peer relationships. Thousands of children ring ChildLine each year asking for advice on bullying and social exclusion (ChildLine 2005). The UK Children's Commissioner describes his role as that of a children's champion by standing up for children's views and interests in order to improve their lives. On the basis of regular talks with children throughout the UK, he asked children to help him identify the issues of greatest concern. The theme that attracted the greatest attention was bullying (Aynsley-Green 2006). In the extensive overview of the nature of bullying and the range of interventions that exist to counteract it, he especially selected methods that involved young people themselves within the context of a whole-school policy as being those with the greatest impact. One of the justifications that he gave for peer support as a valuable intervention was that it involves not only the bully and the victim, but also the bystanders who are potentially in a position to challenge bullying as soon as it occurs. Furthermore, the presence of an effective peer support system in a school is likely to strengthen the school community as a whole.

Peer support training involves the enhancement of qualities such as active listening, empathy, a problem-solving stance and the capacity to see things from different perspectives. This position ties in with research in the field of emotional intelligence which demonstrates the positive impact that an emotionally literate environment can have. Harris (2000) showed that children who score highly on their ability to identify and interpret emotions – skills that peer supporters learn and practise in the course of their training – are better at developing and sustaining interpersonal relationships. Frey *et al.*, (2005), Grossman *et al.*, (1997) and Van Schoiack Edstrom *et al.*, (2002) have shown the positive impact of emotional literacy programmes on the quality of interpersonal relationships at school. Schools that use these programmes also report on reductions in aggressive behaviour.

Peer support programmes have become more popular internationally in schools as interventions that promote the United Nations Convention on the Rights of the Child (1989) and have the potential to improve pupil safety, to enhance emotional health and well-being and to combat school violence and bullying (Cowie *et al.* 2004). Peer support builds on the willingness of most young people to act in a co-operative, friendly way towards one another. Peer support schemes, in a range of forms, build on this natural friendliness and create structures that facilitate young people's potential for responsibility, caring and empathy for others.

Primary school schemes generally involve training certain pupils as *buddies* or *befrienders*. Peer supporters are trained to look out for pupils that appear lonely, often in the playground, and to offer friendly contact; they also report serious fights and conflicts to adults. There may be a 'buddy bench' where pupils can go in the playground if they would like peer support. In addition some primary schools incorporate other activities for peer supporters, such as leading games activities, supporting learning at a homework club, and one-to-one work with very young pupils who need support in learning how to be friends with others. Secondary school peer support schemes usually involve *peer mentors*, who may offer support to pupils with difficulties in a 'drop in' room, help primary school pupils make the transition to secondary school, do group work with a tutor group, offer one-to-one contact with a pupil in need over a period of time, or run a lunchtime club for younger pupils (Andrès 2007; Cowie *et al.* 2002; Cowie and Wallace 2000; Smith and Watson 2004). Peer supporters can also be elected by their peers to deal with interpersonal issues (Andrès 2007). Some secondary school pupils work as mediators to resolve conflicts through a structured process to resolve disputes (Cremin 2007; Fernandez, Villaoslada and Funes 2002; Stacey and Robinson 2003).

Peer support is not about giving advice. Rather it involves training pupils to listen to their peers, responding genuinely and authentically to the needs and feelings of those seeking help and liaising with appropriate adults when necessary. This is where good communication skills, emotional literacy and a problem-solving stance are essential. There should also be some form of supervision and debriefing by adults (usually the co-ordinator of the peer support system) to allow time for peer supporters to process what they do and collectively to address the issues that they encounter.

Most recently, with technological advances, the internet offers new directions for the development of peer support interventions, including use of the internet and e-mail support (Cartwright 2005; Cowie and Hutson 2005; Hutson and Cowie 2007). Peer supporters in the UK have begun to develop systems that ensure confidentiality by working anonymously through their school's intranet (Cartwright 2005; Cowie and Hutson 2005; Hutson and Cowie 2007). Such systems reach vulnerable young people who might otherwise stay silent about their distress, and are especially attractive to young people who might otherwise fear that their issues will not be treated in confidence. Typically, small groups of peer supporters work together on a rota system to respond to e-mails during certain time slots so that everyone who uses the system will receive a reasonably quick response. Cowie and Jennifer (2007) comment on the potential that *cyber peer support* has for offering young people resources and information on useful strategies and help lines and provide case studies of its use in practice.

HOW EFFECTIVE ARE PEER SUPPORT SYSTEMS?

Cowie and Smith (in press) reviewed three main outcomes of peer support schemes:

- outcomes for peer supporters
- outcomes for users of peer support systems
- outcomes for the school ethos in general.

Outcomes for peer supporters

Evaluations of peer support schemes have consistently indicated certain advantages of peer support for those who are trained to implement the schemes. Benefits reported by peer supporters include: being more confident; developing a sense of responsibility; valuing people more; feeling gratification at doing something to help improve the quality of life in their school community; satisfaction at learning skills such as conflict resolution (Cowie 1998; Cowie *et al.* 2002; Naylor and Cowie 1999). At the same time, some peer supporters report difficulties that include: hostility on the part of peers, with boys especially vulnerable to taunts about their masculinity; jealousy because of their role or because of the attention received from the school, the community or even the media; undervaluing of their skills by some staff (Andrès 2007; Naylor and Cowie 1999; Smith and Watson 2004). In some very violent contexts, peer supporters report feeling overwhelmed by the magnitude of the task that they felt they were expected to do (Cowie and Olafsson 2001).

Overall, despite the difficulties reported by some peer supporters, on the basis of this evidence about the impact of peer support systems on peer helpers, Cowie and Smith (in press) conclude that the practice of peer support appears to give direction to some young people's altruistic wishes to address injustices such as bullying and deliberate social exclusion in their school community, and that the training enhances their communication and problem-solving skills and their capacity to feel empathy for peers in distress. There is also informal evidence that peer supporters' career goals are clarified through experiences of helping others and that interview panels regularly express interest in this aspect of a young person's CV.

Outcomes for users of peer support systems

A number of studies have interviewed or surveyed pupils who have used peer support systems and have asked them how satisfied they were with the quality of the service they received. On the whole, reports are positive for those pupils who actually use the systems. For example, Naylor and Cowie (1999) found that 82 per cent of users reported that they found peer support 'useful' or 'very useful'; 82 per cent said that they found these helpful in giving them the strength to cope with bullying; and 80 per cent said that they would recommend the system to a friend. In the follow-up study two years later, Cowie *et al.* (2002) confirmed these findings; overall, 87 per cent of bullied pupils said that the system had been useful or very useful to them, the most frequent reason given being that it helps to talk to a peer. Even in the adverse circumstances of the underprivileged school investigated by Cowie and Olafsson (2001), the majority of users reported that they valued having a peer to listen to their problems, and found it helpful to have the protection of a peer supporter's presence. Similar levels of satisfaction were reported by Smith and Watson (2004) who found that 44 per cent of primary school users said it helped a lot, 50 per cent said it helped a bit, and only 6 per cent that it did not help. Cowie and Smith (in press) conclude that the majority of users report finding the schemes helpful.

Outcomes for school ethos

Teachers frequently report that the school environment becomes safer and more caring following the introduction of a peer support scheme, and that peer relationships in general improve (Cowie *et al.* 2002; Cowie and Sharp 1996; Cremin 2007; Hurst 2001; Mental Health Foundation 2002; Naylor and Cowie 1999; Smith and Watson 2004). Lane-Garon and Richardson (2003) studied the impact of a peer mediation scheme on school climate in a sample of 300 elementary school pupils in the US. Both mediators and non-mediators perceived the school climate to be safer than had been reported in the year prior to the introduction of the peer mediation scheme. This represented an increase from 56 per cent (in 1999) to 66 per cent (in 2001) of pupils who either agreed or strongly agreed that they felt safe on campus. Responses to the items *Other students treat me with respect at school*, and *I feel like I belong here*, both increased from 47 per cent to 58 per cent over this period. However, other studies have been less positive in this domain. Naylor and Cowie (1999) found that peer support systems did not appear to reduce bullying, since its incidence as measured by an anonymous questionnaire was similar to that reported in other surveys at that time (e.g. Whitney and Smith 1993). Nevertheless, on the basis of users' responses to their questionnaire, they argued that the presence of a peer support system reduced the negative impact of bullying on victims and made it more acceptable for them to report it, especially as it was perceived by both users and potential users that peers are able to detect bullying at a much earlier stage than adults can.

Investigations into pupil reports on experiences and perceptions of safety at school reveal some challenging findings when similar schools, those with and those without a peer support system in place, are compared (Cowie and Oztug 2008). Salmivalli (2001) reported mixed effects of a small-scale peer-led intervention in a Finnish secondary school, of a general awareness-raising nature. Seventh- and eight-graders (13–15 years) were assessed. For seventh-grade girls there were positive outcomes (reduction in self- and peer-reports of victimization), but these were not found in eighth-grade girls, or either year group of boys. Girls showed an increase in willingness to influence bullying problems; but boys actually increased in pro-bullying attitudes. However, this intervention was very short and there was no control group comparison. Cowie and Olafsson (2001), in their study of one secondary school with high levels of violence, administered the Olweus bullying questionnaire (1996) before the introduction of the peer support service and 7.5 months after. The high incidence of bullying in the school showed little change over the period when the peer support service was in operation. When asked how often teachers, peer supporters and other young people tried to put a stop to someone being bullied, pupils tended to perceive all three parties as intervening less in June than in the previous November. Similarly, Andrès (2007) had mixed results in her comparison of two schools, one with experimental peer support and one without peer support in place. She found that rates of physical bullying increased in the experimental school, as did the incidence of aggressive conflicts. However, she found that social exclusion decreased in the experimental school, suggesting that peer support interventions could have a positive impact on psychological forms of bullying.

Cowie *et al.* (2008) surveyed around 900 secondary school pupils in total, and found that the pupils in the peer support schools reported feeling no safer in the toilets, the playground, corridors and in lessons than their counterparts in the non-peer support control schools. However, it appeared that a substantial minority of pupils were unaware of the presence of the peer support systems. When the pupils who were not aware of the peer support system (NAPS) were compared with pupils who were aware (APS), the researchers found that the pupils who were not aware of their school's peer support system were significantly more likely to worry a lot about being bullied than those who were aware. The APS felt significantly safer in lessons and were more likely to view school as friendly place to be. The APS pupils were also significantly more likely to tell someone when bad things happened to them, such as being bullied, and even to confide in someone (usually a member of their family or a close friend) if they themselves had done something unpleasant to another person. The authors suggest that the awareness that there are other pupils in the school to offer help, should they need it, enables pupils to create a construction of school as a safe place to be. This is confirmed by the finding that they are prepared to confide in someone when they themselves transgress. In other words, the APS pupils have internalized the idea that it is helpful to share worries, anxieties and feelings of guilt with another person.

DISCUSSION OF FINDINGS

The most well-established findings concern the benefits of peer support systems for the peer supporters, which have been nearly universally reported in the studies reviewed. These benefits probably stem from the quality of training and supervision received, and the practice of skills in a context generally valued by other pupils and the school. Users also report benefits, with only a minority saying that peer support is unhelpful. It is also worth noting that a proportion of former victims of bullying are consistently present among the ranks of peer supporters, demonstrating the value of peer support training and practice in restoring the self-esteem and confidence of vulnerable pupils in the context of a supportive, well-motivated group.

However, the extent of the impact of peer support systems on the general climate of school is less clearly documented. There are subjective impressions that school ethos improves and that rates of bullying decrease, but objective, unbiased evidence of such improvements is less frequent. The studies that have carried out direct comparisons between schools with and those without a peer support system in place indicate that it is not enough to train a cohort of pupils in peer support methods. It is essential to continue to advertise the service and promote it to widen potential participation as much as possible. Cowie and

Oztug (2008) recommend that peer support training should also include some peer research knowledge and skills so that peer supporters can carry out regular evaluations of the effectiveness of their schemes. They also suggest that there should be a greater encouragement to consult with the school population to identify what their social and emotional needs actually are, as Aynsley-Green (2006) did on his appointment to the position of Children's Commissioner in the UK.

Research into peer support illustrates the on-going difficulty involved in measuring the processes that take place when people intervene to change behaviour and attitudes. Too often in this field, evaluation is provided by practitioners who have established peer support in their own school or by entrepreneurs who have a vested interest in promoting their own methods of intervention. Those studies that evaluate peer support using more rigorous methods tend to measure outcomes, such as reduction in rates of bullying and incidence of conflicts and increase in pupil perceptions of safety. There is a need to develop a wider range of studies that explore the processes of change both in those who participate (whether users or helpers) and in the wider school population. There is a need for rigorous research that combines quantitative and qualitative methods to capture the complexity of the changes that peer support potentially promotes, and to unravel the complex social processes involved. There is also a need to involve young people themselves, perhaps as peer researchers, in order to gain richer insights into the ways that peer supporters might influence relationships in the peer group and the techniques that have greatest impact (Veale 2005).

Peer support is one of the most rapidly growing forms of intervention in the struggle against school violence and bullying. The research to date has indicated some very promising outcomes. However, there is a need for more meticulous studies of the processes involved through observations of peer support in action, through peer-led reflections on the experience of peer support, and other innovative methods.

REFERENCES

Andrès, S. (2007) *Los sistemas de ayuda entre iguales como instrumentos de mejora de la convivencia en la escuela: Evaluacion de una intervención.* Unpublished PhD thesis, Universidad Autonoma, Madrid.

Aynsley-Green, A. (2006) *Bullying Today.* London: Office of the Children's Commissioner.

Cartwright, N. (2005) 'Setting up and sustaining peer support systems in a range of schools over 20 years.' *Pastoral Care in Education 23,* 45–50.

ChildLine (2005) *Every School Should Have One: How Peer Support Schemes Make Schools Better.* London: ChildLine.

Cowie, H. (1998) 'Perspective of teachers and pupils on the experience of peer support against bullying.' *Educational Research and Evaluation 4,* 108–125.

Cowie, H., Boardman, C., Dawkins, J. and Jennifer, D. (2004) *Emotional Health and Well-being: A Practical Guide for Schools.* London: Sage.

Cowie, H. and Hutson, N. (2005) 'Peer support: A strategy to help bystanders challenge school bullying.' *Pastoral Care in Education 23,* 40–44.

Cowie, H., Hutson, N., Oztug, O. and Myers, C. (2008) 'The impact of peer support schemes on pupils' perceptions of bullying, aggression and safety at school.' *Emotional and Behavioural Difficulties 13,* 1, 63–71.

Cowie, H. and Jennifer, D. (2007) *Violence in Schools: A Whole-School Approach to Best Practice.* London: Sage.

Cowie, H., Naylor, P., Talamelli, L., Chauhan, P. and Smith, P.K. (2002) 'Knowledge, use of and attitudes towards peer support.' *Journal of Adolescence 25,* 453–467.

Cowie, H. and Olafsson, R. (2001) 'The role of peer support in helping the victims of bullying in a school with high levels of aggression.' *School Psychology International 21,* 79–95.

Cowie, H. and Oztug, O. (2008) 'Pupils' perceptions of safety at school.' *Pastoral Care in Education 26,* 59–67.

Cowie, H. and Sharp, S. (1996) *Peer Counselling in Schools: A Time to Listen.* London: David Fulton.

Cowie, H. and Smith, P.K. (in press) 'Peer Support as a Means of Improving School Safety and Reducing Bullying and Violence.' In B. Doll, J. Charvat, J. Baker and G. Stoner (eds) *Handbook of Prevention Research.* Mahwah, NJ: Lawrence Erlbaum.

Cowie, H. and Wallace, P. (2000) *Peer Support in Action.* London: Sage.

Cremin, H. (2007) *Peer Mediation.* London: Open University Press.

Fernandez, I., Villaoslada, E. and Funes, S. (2002) *Conflicto en el Centro Escolar.* Madrid: Catarata.

Frey, K.S., Nolen, S.B., Van Schoiack Edstrom, L. and Hirschstein, M.K. (2005) 'Effects of a school-based social-emotional competence program: Linking children's goals, attributions, and behavior.' *Applied Developmental Psychology 26,* 171–200.

Grossman, C.D., Neckerman, H.J., Koepsell, T.D., Liu, P.Y., Ashere, K., Beland, K., Frey, K. and Rivara, F.P. (1997) 'Effectiveness of a violence prevention curriculum among children in elementary school: A randomized controlled trial.' *Journal of the American Medical Association 277,* 1605–1611.

Harris, P.L. (2000) 'Understanding Emotion.' In M. Lewis and J. Haviland-Jones (eds) *Handbook of Emotions* (2nd edition., pp.281–292). New York: Guilford Press.

Hurst, T. (2001) 'An evaluation of an anti-bullying peer support programme in a British secondary school.' *Pastoral Care in Education 19,* 10–14.

Hutson, N. and Cowie, H. (2007) 'Setting up an e-mail peer support scheme.' *Pastoral Care in Education, 25,* 12–16.

Lane-Garon, P. and Richardson, T. (2003) 'Mediator mentors: Improving school climate – nurturing student disposition.' *Conflict Resolution Quarterly 21,* 47–69.

Mental Health Foundation (2002) *Peer support: Someone to turn to. An Evaluation Report of the Mental Health Foundation Peer Support Programme.* London and Glasgow: Mental Health Foundation.

Naylor, P. and Cowie, H. (1999) 'The effectiveness of peer support systems in challenging school bullying: The perspectives and experiences of teachers and pupils.' *Journal of Adolescence 22,* 467–479.

Olweus, D. (1996) *The Revised Olweus Bully/Victim Questionnaire.* Bergen: Research Center for Health Promotion, University of Bergen.

Salmivalli, C. (2001) 'Peer-led intervention campaign against school bullying: Who considered it useful, who benefited?' *Educational Research 43,* 263–278.

Smith, P.K. and Watson, D. (2004) *Evaluation of the CHIPS (ChildLine in Partnership with Schools) Programme.* Research report RR570. Nottingham: DfES Publications.

Stacey, H. and Robinson, P. (2003) *Let's Mediate: A Teacher's Guide to Peer Support and Conflict Resolution Skills for All Ages.* Bristol: Lucky Duck Publications.

Veale, A. (2005) 'Creative Methodologies in Participatory Research with Children.' In S. Greene and D. Hogan (eds) *Researching Children's Experience* (pp.253–272). London: Sage.

Van Schoiack Edstrom, L., Frey, K.S. and Beland, K. (2002) 'Changing adolescents' attitudes about relational and physical aggression: An early evaluation of a school-based intervention.' *School Psychology Review 31,* 2, 201–216.

Whitney, I. and Smith, P.K. (1993) 'A survey of the nature and extent of bully/victim problems in junior/middle and secondary schools.' *Educational Research 35,* 3–25.

CHAPTER 7

Classwide Peer Tutoring and Students with SEBD

Anastasia Karagiannakis
and Ingrid Sladeczek

INTRODUCTION

Students exhibiting social, emotional and behaviour difficulties (SEBD) are of great concern to their teachers, parents, peers, and to themselves (Beebe-Frankenberger *et al.* 2005; Hollinger 1987; Vidoni, Fleming and Mintz 1983). Numerous attempts have been undertaken to facilitate the learning experience for such students who attend special education classes or schools. However, for students with SEBD attending regular education classrooms, the learning process continues to be a cause for concern for teachers and students themselves. Effective and early interventions that address students' needs in such settings are critical; without such interventions, the students are susceptible to continued behaviour problems, as their profile is indicative of continued social, emotional and behavioural difficulties (Lochman *et al.* 2006; Stacks 2005) and academic failure (Lopes 2005; McLeod and Kaiser 2004; Tewhey 2006). One of these interventions is peer tutoring, and this chapter describes a study which has examined the effectiveness of classwide peer tutoring in the education of students with social, emotional and behaviour difficulties.

CLASSWIDE PEER TUTORING

Peer tutoring has been positively correlated with enhanced academic, behavioural and social functioning of students with SEBD, whether in the role of tutors or tutees (Cohen, Kulik, and Kulik 1982; Durrer and McLaughlin 1995;

King 2007; Scruggs, Mastropieri and Richter 1985). In particular, classwide peer tutoring (CWPT) (Greenwood, Delquadri and Carta 1997) is an intervention programme that has been researched over the past 25 years and has been found to have a positive impact on the academic and socio-emotional functioning of students both with and without individual educational needs (e.g. Bell *et al.* 1990; Hughes and Fredrick 2006; Plumer and Stoner 2005; Utley *et al.* 2001). CWPT is an educational programme with behaviour management components, including reinforcement of correct behaviour, child recognition and praise, peer-mediated contingencies (i.e. as tutors, children are trained to award contingent points, to use error correction procedures), and the use of feedback on individual and group performance. Students have the opportunity to respond to questions by allowing peers to supervise their responses, and there are frequent interactions between the tutors and the tutees, which are necessary conditions for academic achievement (e.g. Delquadri *et al.* 1986; Maheady *et al.* 2004). In this way, the entire classroom is involved without stigmatising and pointing out children with SEBD.

In a CWPT session, a class is typically divided into two teams that engage in competitions for a one- to two-week period. Following a structured, teacher-developed lesson, the students tutor one another on the same material. The tutor presents an instructional item and the tutee says and writes the response. The tutor reinforces correct responses and corrects errors. Each pair accumulates points for their team (which consists of half of the students in the classroom) by responding correctly during the session. At the end of the one- to two-week competition, a test is administered to assess the skills learned and additional points are awarded to the teams accordingly. Each team's points are totalled, and the winning team is announced.

The implementation of CWPT results in an immediate and substantial increase in the weekly test scores and an improvement in the basic academic skills performance of students with and without individual educational needs (e.g. Hughes and Fredrick 2006; Plumer and Stoner 2005; Utley *et al.* 2001). This intervention is different from traditional classroom instruction as students have the opportunity to respond to questions by allowing peers to supervise their interventions, and there are frequent interactions between the tutors and tutees, which are necessary conditions for academic achievement (Delquadri *et al.* 1986; Maheady, Mallette and Harper 2006). CWPT is also dependent on behaviour analysis principles, including reinforcing clear presentation of materials and correct responses, recognition and praise of individual responses, and providing feedback on individual and group performance. It is a very flexible and adaptable approach, and it fits into the teacher's current teaching method, style and educational programme. It is cost-effective, with no extra materials to purchase; it supplements the texts or materials the teacher is currently using. The programme is easy to implement. Once a teacher has taught students the roles of tutors and tutees, the students can then run the programme on their own. CWPT is also time-efficient; it can be implemented in 30 to 35-minute blocks. Moreover, as students become more proficient, time decreases. More importantly, CWPT increases the students' active exposure to the content, multiplying the opportunities students have to respond (Greenwood *et al.* 1997).

This chapter provides the findings of a study that investigated boys' academic performance, on-task behaviour, self-concept, and satisfaction, following a 12-week CWPT programme. The objectives of the study were to examine:

- the spelling and mathematics achievement of boys who participate or do not participate in CWPT

- the academic, social, behavioural, and global self-concept of boys who do or do not participate in CWPT

- the on-task behaviour of boys with and without SEBD who are or are not participating in CWPT.

METHODOLOGY

The CWPT group, in Montreal, Canada, included 20 boys with SEBD and 20 boys without such difficulties (age 8 to 11 years old). The control group, which did not receive the CWPT intervention, consisted of 14 boys with SEBD and 19 boys without. Both groups were tested at pre- and post-intervention. A battery of tests was used to measure whether significant changes in academic achievement, self-concept, and on-task behaviour occurred following the 12-week intervention.

Participating schools were randomly assigned to either experimental or control schools. The first school (experimental group, $N = 175$) included boys with and without SEBD who participated in the CWPT programme. The second school (control group, $N = 166$) included boys with and without SEBD who did not receive any CWPT. Teachers and students received two days of training in implementing the CWPT programme. The programme required approximately 30 minutes of implementation each day and was implemented on a four-day cycle. On the first day, a pre-test was given to children on the spelling words or mathematical concepts to be learned during the week. Teachers introduced the new content and students tutored each other three times a week. Students were randomly paired in the classroom for one week, forming two teams. In each team, students took turns in tutoring their partner in spelling or mathematics for a total of 20 minutes. Tutors presented an instructional item and the tutees said and wrote the responses. The tutors reinforced correct responses and corrected errors.

RESULTS AND DISCUSSION
Spelling and mathematics
Weekly spelling and mathematics performance
Important gains were achieved for boys with SEBD in the CWPT programme, as their aggregate weekly spelling and mathematics scores significantly increased by about 50 points in each case from pre- to post-testing (Figures 7.1 and 7.2). This is an important finding because boys made gains in a short period of time given that the classwide peer tutoring occurred for a total of one hour per week. It is well established that boys with behaviour problems (BP) tend to underachieve academically primarily due to disruptive and off-task behaviours (Gest and Gest 2005). In comparison, boys without SEBD in the CWPT programme improved their aggregate spelling and mathematics scores by about 40 points in each case, even though their pre-test scores were higher than those of the boys with SEBD. In sharp contrast, no significant improvement in these two areas was observed in any of the boys in the control group, particularly boys with SEBD. In contrast, although an improvement in the areas of spelling and mathematics was observed for boys with and without SEBD in the control group, their improvement was not as high as the significant improvements observed in the CWPT condition. However, in the SEBD control group there was a high improvement in the maths scores from pre- to post-intervention. One possible explanation for this significant improvement could be the pedagogy used by the teacher. It is possible that the students responded favourably to this particular approach (e.g. students working in groups of three or four, maths games) as opposed to the more traditional teaching methods (e.g. independent work, large group instruction). Nevertheless, although there was a significant improvement, the difference was not as high as that of the CWPT group.

These results strongly support the notion that a peer can take on the role of a teacher to teach specific concepts in a structured manner. More importantly, the one-to-one individualized learning time that boys received were important components in the boys' successful post-test performance. These findings extend the positive academic outcomes to a new population of children, namely SEBD. Previous researchers have examined the academic performance of students with and without individual educational needs and have found positive results following the implementation of CWPT. This was the first study to examine the spelling and mathematics performance of boys with SEBD in inclusive classrooms.

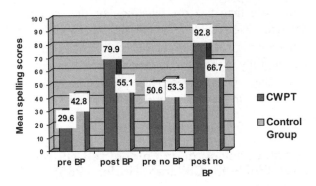

Figure 7.1: Spelling performance in boys' weekly tests from pre- to post-intervention

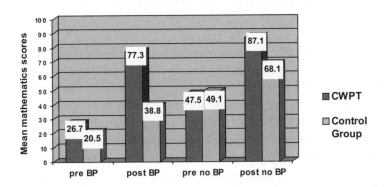

Figure 7.2: Mathematics performance in boys' weekly tests from pre- to post-intervention

WRAT-3 results

Post-intervention improvements on the Wide Range Achievement Test-3 (Wilkinson 1993), a standardized achievement test measuring reading, spelling and arithmetic, were observed in the spelling sub-scale (Figure 7.3). Significant improvements were also observed in the arithmetic sub-scale for boys with SEBD in the CWPT intervention (Figure 7.4). Unexpected significant improvements in the reading sub-scale of the WRAT-3 were also found for this group (Figure 7.5). This finding may suggest that the CWPT intervention tapped into more than just the repetition of the spelling words or mathematical steps to solve a problem. Specifically, boys were required to read the spelling words and the mathematical problem-solving examples to engage actively and meaningfully in the tutoring experience and produce the significant improvements that were achieved. These are important findings as it is well established that such improvements are usually obtained over one scholastic year period.

Academic, social, behavioural and global self-concept (Self-perception Profile for Children: Harter 1985)

Academic self-concept

Boys with SEBD in the CWPT intervention group achieved significant gains in their academic self-concept from pre- to post-intervention (Figure 7.6). In contrast, boys with SEBD in the control school, reported a higher academic self-concept at pre-intervention but lower academic self-concept at post-intervention when compared to the boys with SEBD who participated in the CWPT. Similarly, boys without SEBD who participated in CWPT made significant gains in their academic self-concept, compared to their matched participants.

It is hypothesized that the small decrease in the academic self-concept of boys in the non-CWPT group can be due to the boys' perceptions of minimal improvements on the spelling and mathematics tasks. As there were no rewards or special activities associated with the tutoring experience in the non-CWPT group, it is possible that the students' views of their academic abilities did not change. Please note: although there is a decrease in academic self-concept based on the statistical analyses this is not a significant decrease, indicating that the self-concept was similar at pre- and post-intervention.

These findings provide strong support for the implementation of CWPT as an academic intervention that can increase the academic self-concept of boys SEBD. This improvement in self-concept can be directly related to the boys' improvements in their weekly and post-intervention spelling and

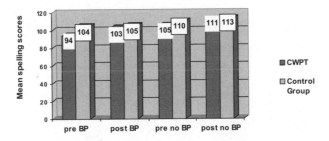

Figure 7.3: Spelling performance of boys on the WRAT-3 standardized measure

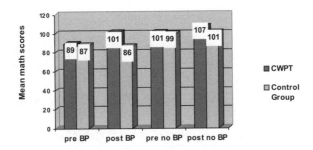

Figure 7.4: Mathematics performance of boys on the WRAT-3 standardized measure

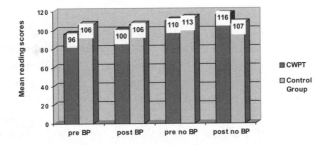

Figure 7.5: Reading performance of boys on the WRAT-3 standardized measure

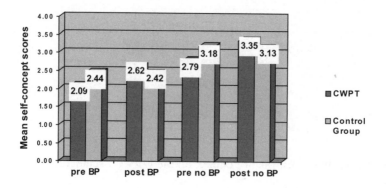

Figure 7.6: Academic self-concept of boys from pre- to post-intervention

mathematics performance. Although there was a slight decrease in the academic self-concept of students in the control group, the decrease was not significant, indicating that the academic self-concept of students in this group was similar at pre- and post-intervention. Thus, the boys' reports of their academic self-concept appear to be directly related to the weekly spelling and mathematics scores and the significant improvements on the standardized measure in mathematics. This is an important finding that needs to be replicated, as this is the first study to examine the self-concept of boys with SEBD following the CWPT implementation.

Behavioural and social self-concept

Boys with SEBD reported significant improvements in their behaviour and social skills following their participation in CWPT (Figures 7.7 and 7.8). This finding is corroborated by parental and teacher reports of decreased externalizing and internalizing behaviours, and an observed improvement in the boys' social skills. The significant improvements in the boys' perceptions of their behavioural and social skills can attest to the efficacy of the CWPT programme in having an indirect positive impact on the students' behaviour. Only recently have secondary gains (i.e. other than academic improvements) been investigated with children with individual educational needs. In the non-CWPT group, a decrease in the behavioural self-concept was observed. The primary objective of CWPT is to enhance the academic performance of children; secondary gains, such as improvements in behaviour or social skills

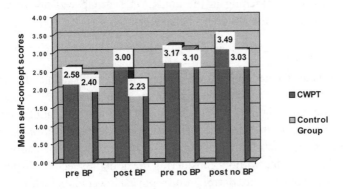

Figure 7.7: Behavioural conduct self-concept of boys from pre- to post-intervention

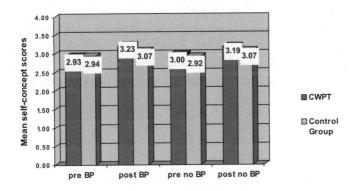

Figure 7.8: Social self-concept of boys from pre- to post-intervention

have recently been investigated with children who have special needs. Since the non-CWPT group were not exposed to the behaviour management components of the experimental group, including reinforcement for correct behaviour, recognition and praise, peer-mediated strategies (students trained as tutors awarding points for correct responses) and feedback on individual and group performance, changes in behaviour were not to be expected. A decrease in behavioural self-concept may therefore have resulted from the fact that the focus of the teaching in the non-CWPT group was not primarily directed to improving the children's behaviour.

Global self-concept

All boys who participated in the CWPT intervention, both with and without SEBD, reported significant improvements in their global self-concept following the programme (Figure 7.9). This finding is in line with that of previous researchers who hypothesized that self-concept is defined in a uni-dimensional manner, in which individuals generally report positive perceptions in their overall functioning without considering the domain-specific self-perceptions. The SEBD boys in the control group reported lower global self-concepts at pre-intervention in comparison to the SEBD boys who participated in the CWPT intervention. It is possible that the boys in the non-CWPT group perceived their overall functioning accurately and were more aware of their difficulties. In contrast, it is also possible that the boys in the CWPT group perceived their overall functioning positively, but they were able to pinpoint their areas of difficulty in other areas of domain-specific self-concept (for example, academic, social, behavioural). In addition, at pre-intervention, the global self-concept of the non-SEBD boys in the control group was higher than that of their counterparts; however, it did not change significantly, whereas the global self-concept of non-SEBD boys in the CWPT condition improved significantly. This improvement can be attributed to the fact that although these

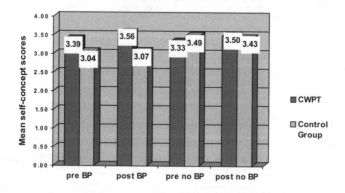

Figure 7.9: Global self-concept of boys from pre- to post-intervention

students did not have behaviour problems, they appreciated the components of the CWPT programme and responded to them positively.

The measure employed in the study to investigate domain-specific self-perceptions was an important strength which could explain the differences between the experimental and the control groups. As it taps into the multidimensionality of self-concept, specific domains in which the boys' self-concepts improved were easily identifiable. It is difficult to change global self-concept in a short period of time, and, more so, to change domain-specific self-perceptions. However, when targeting specific self-concept domains, improvements can be observed. For example, if students improve their behavioural and academic performance, then their behavioural and academic self-concepts will likely improve as well. In this study, an improvement in the academic, behavioural, and social self-concepts was targeted for students with SEBD as a result of their participation in the CWPT. As a result, significant improvements in particular domains of self-concept for boys with SEBD were noted, which appears to be associated with a concurrent improvement in their academic, behavioural, and social skills functioning.

On-task behaviours (Direct Observation Form: Achenback and Edelbrock 1986)

On-task behaviour

Significant improvements were observed in the on-task behaviours (e.g. following directions, working at one's desk, working cooperatively) of boys with SEBD from Time 1 (no CWPT) to Time 2 (mid-point during CWPT). More importantly, the gains were maintained when their behaviour was observed at Time 3, two weeks after cessation of CWPT (Figure 7.10). The highest on-task behaviour occurred during Time 2. There were added opportunities to practise the spelling and mathematics concepts being tutored, and the information was presented at a rapid pace so that on-task behaviours could be maintained (e.g. DuPaul et al. 1998; Greenwood, Maheady and Delquadri 2002). When boys are actively involved in their own learning, they usually do not exhibit externalizing difficulties such as aggression and non-compliance simultaneously, as they must be focused on the material to be learned. Further, as CWPT involved reciprocal peer tutoring, boys with SEBD were engaged in the tutor and tutee roles, thus they were required to be on-task throughout the 20-minute sessions in which they were the 'teacher' and the student.

Active and passive on-task behaviour

On-task behaviour was further divided into two types: active and passive. Active on-task behaviour includes behaviours that students must be actively involved in to be on-task, such as writing their responses, reading the words from the tutoring list, or awarding points to their partner. On the other hand, passive on-task behaviours include behaviours such as listening to instructions from the tutor. In both instances, students are demonstrating on-task behaviours; some may be active and others passive.

All boys in the CWPT programme showed significant improvements in their active on-task behaviour from Time 1 to Time 2. The active on-task behaviour was however, not maintained at Time 3, two weeks following cessation of CWPT, which can be due to the boys engaging in the learning process in a passive manner, such as listening to the teacher or peer presentations. In sharp contrast, all boys in the control group did not show any improvement in their active on-task behaviour, which was significantly lower across the three times in comparison to that of the CWPT boys (Figure 7.11).

The passive on-task behaviour for boys participating in the CWPT intervention was significantly lower than their active on-task behaviour and the passive behaviour of the control boys across Times 1, 2, and 3. This finding suggests that as the boys were actively engaged in CWPT, their time was spent productively teaching and learning the academic content, thus enhancing their active participation in their own learning, which is a prerequisite to enhancing their academic performance (Figure 7.12).

Child satisfaction

All the boys reported that they enjoyed the peer tutoring activity, and the great majority reported that the peer tutor helped them become better students. They enjoyed receiving points for obtaining the correct responses, would like to have a peer tutor again, and would tell their friends to have a peer tutor. Many boys perceived the CWPT experience as a 'learning game' because they learned new spelling words and mathematics in a game format, which was more engaging for them than simply listening to the teacher explaining the material. By the third to fourth week of implementation, the boys had mastered the CWPT principles and were implementing the programme on their own, while the classroom teacher was observing the process and awarding bonus points to the boys who were actively participating in the programme and following the rules of the game.

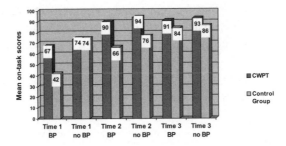

Figure 7.10: On-task behaviour of the boys at three time points

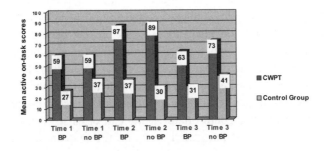

Figure 7.11: Active on-task behaviour of the boys at three time points

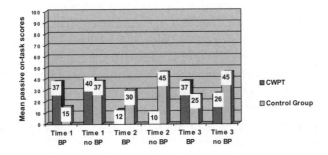

Figure 7.12: Passive on-task behaviour of the boys at three time points

Teacher satisfaction

All the teachers reported that the programme was time- and cost-effective. Many expressed overall satisfaction with the programme and reported that it was beneficial for the students, contributing to significant changes in their academic functioning. They continued to employ peer tutoring procedures with students with SEBD in some form, and recommended it to other mainstream education teachers.

CONCLUSION

The CWPT programme is an excellent alternative to traditional teaching methods. It actively involves all students in the classroom, including boys with SEBD, in the learning process. One of its important strengths is its focus on including students with SEBD in the tutoring process, whether in the role of a tutor or tutee. A major component of the intervention is its reliance on behavioural management principles at the individual and classroom levels, whereby students with SEBD rely on each other's academic and behavioural performance to improve their own academic and behavioural functioning. All students with SEBD are active participants in their own learning as tutees, but are also actively engaged in learning how to teach, correct and praise their peers' accurate responding to questions. Further, the different weekly incentives and certificates they could obtain at the end of each week had a high motivational value. This is particularly relevant for students with SEBD, as they tend to respond favourably to such behaviour management procedures (Smith et al. 2001; Winzer 1999). As teachers in inclusive education classrooms may feel unprepared to meet the needs of students with individual educational needs, particularly those with SEBD (Pivik, McComas and LaFlamme 2002), an attractive quality of peer tutoring is that it 'relies heavily on a relatively abundant resource (i.e. students) and places comparatively modest demands on scarcer resources' (i.e. educators) (Dufrene et al. 2005, p.75). CWPT enables teachers to involve and include all students in the learning process. It facilitates the accommodation of the learning and socio-emotional needs of all students in the inclusive classroom. It helps the mainstream teachers to promote appropriate social interactions and behaviour. Students with SEBD feel better about themselves and are more likely to be accepted by their peers when their social skills improve and their behaviour problems decrease.

Finally, the positive gains resulting from implementation of CWPT highlight the importance for regular and special education teachers to become more informed and proficient in the use of CWPT with boys and girls who have SEBD, and to other groups of students as well. Further, teacher-education programmes should strive to train pre-service and in-service teachers how to implement this promising practice in inclusive classrooms.

REFERENCES

Achenbach, T.M. and Edelbrock, C.S. (1986) *Child Behavior Checklist – Direct Observation Form* (Rev. edition) Burlington, VT: Center for Children, Youth, and Families, University of Vermont.

Beebe-Frankenberger, M., Lane, K.L., Bocian, K.M., Gresham, F.M. and MacMillan, D.L. (2005) 'Students with or at risk for problem behavior: Betwixt and between teacher and parent expectations.' *Preventing School Failure 49*, 10–17.

Bell, K., Young, K.R., Blair, M. and Nelson, R. (1990) 'Facilitating mainstreaming of students with behavioral disorders using classwide peer tutoring.' *School Psychology Review 19*, 564–573.

Cohen, P.A., Kulik, J.A. and Kulik, C.C. (1982) 'Educational outcomes of tutoring: A meta analysis of findings.' *American Educational Research Journal 19*, 237–248.

Delquadri, J., Greenwood, C.R., Whorton, D., Carta, J.J. and Hall, R.V. (1986) 'Classwide peer tutoring.' *Exceptional Children 52*, 535–542.

Dufrene, B.A., Noell, G.H., Gibertson, D.N. and Duhon, G.J. (2005) 'Monitoring implementation of reciprocal peer tutoring: Identifying and intervening with students who do not maintain accurate implementation.' *School Psychology Review 34*, 74–86.

DuPaul, G.J., Ervin, R.A., Hook, C.L. and McGoey, K.E. (1998) 'Peer tutoring for children with attention deficit hyper-activity disorder: Effects on classroom behavior and academic performance.' *Journal of Applied Behavior Analysis 31*, 579–592.

Durrer, B. and McLaughlin, T.F. (1995) 'The use of peer tutoring interventions involving students with behavior disorders.' *B.C. Journal of Special Education 19*, 20–27.

Gest, S.D. and Gest, J.M. (2005) 'Reading tutoring for students at academic and behavioural risk: Effects on time on task in the classroom.' *Education and Treatment of Children 28*, 1–22.

Greenwood, C.R., Delquadri, J.C. and Carta, J.J. (1997) *Together We Can! Classwide Peer Tutoring for Basic Academic Skills*. Longmont, CO: Sopris West.

Greenwood, C.R., Maheady, L. and Delquadri, J. (2002) 'Classwide Peer Tutoring Programs.' In M.R. Shinn, H.M. Walker and G. Stoner (eds) *Interventions for Academic and Behavior Problems II: Preventive and Remedial Approaches* (pp.611–649). Washington, DC: National Association of School Psychologists.

Harter, S. (1985) *Manual for the Self-Perception Profile for Children*. Denver, CO: University of Denver Press.

Hollinger, J.D. (1987) 'Social skills for behaviorally disordered children as preparation for mainstreaming: Theory, practice, and new directions.' *Remedial and Special Education 8*, 17–27.

Hughes, T.A. and Frederick, L.D. (2006) 'Teaching vocabulary with students with learning disabilities using Classwide Peer Tutoring and constant time delay.' *Journal of Behavioral Education 15*, 1–23.

King, J.A. (2007) 'Reciprocal peer tutoring for children with severe emotional, behavioral and learning problems.' *Dissertation Abstracts International Section A: Humanities and Social Sciences 67*, 7-A, 2464.

Lochman, J.E.P., Powell, N.R., Jackson, M.F. and Czopp, W. (2006) 'Cognitive-Behavioral Psychotherapy for Conduct Disorder: The Coping Power Program.' In W.M. Nelson, A.J. Finch and K.J. Hart (eds) *Conduct Disorders: A Practitioner's Guide to Comparative Treatments* (pp.177–215). New York: Springer Publishing.

Lopes, J. (2005) 'Intervention with students with learning, emotional, and behavioral disorders: Why do we take so long to do it?' *Education and Treatment of Children 28*, 345–360.

Maheady, L., Harper, G.F., Mallette, B. and Karnes, M. (2004) 'Preparing preservice teachers to implement Classwide Peer Tutoring.' *Teacher Education and Special Education 27*, 408–418.

Maheady, L., Mallette, B. and Harper, G. (2006) 'Four classwide peer tutoring models: Similarities, differences, and implementation for research and practice.' *Reading and Writing Quarterly: Overcoming Learning Difficulties 22*, 65–89.

McLeod, J.D. and Kaiser, K. (2004) 'Childhood emotional and behavioral problems and educational attainment.' *American Sociological Review 69*, 636–658.

Pivik, J., McComas, J. and LaFlamme, M. (2002) 'Barriers and facilitators to inclusive education.' *Exceptional Children 69*, 97–107.

Plumer, P.J. and Stoner, G. (2005) 'The relative effects of Classwide Peer Tutoring and peer coaching on the positive social behaviors of children with ADHD.' *Journal of Attention Disorders 9*, 290–300.

Scruggs, T.E., Mastropieri, M.A. and Richter, L. (1985) 'Peer tutoring with behaviorally disordered students: Social and academic benefits.' *Behavioral Disorders, 10*, 4, 283–294.

Smith, T.E.C., Polloway, E.A., Patton, J.R., Dowdy, C.A. and Heath, N.L. (2001) *Teaching Students with Special Needs in Inclusive Settings*. Toronto: Pearson Education.

Stacks, A.M. (2005) 'Using an ecological framework for understanding and treating externalizing behavior in early childhood.' *Early Childhood Education Journal 32*, 269–278.

Tewhey, K. (2006) 'Children's support services: Providing a system of care for urban preschoolers with significant behavioral challenges.' *Childhood Education 82*, 289.

Utley, C.A., Reddy, S.S., Delquadri, J.C., Greenwood, C.R., Mortweet, S.L. and Bowman, V. (2001) 'Classwide peer tutoring: An effective teaching procedure for facilitating the acquisition of health education and safety facts with students with developmental disabilities.' *Education and Treatment of Children 24*, 1–27.

Vidoni, D.O., Fleming, N.J. and Mintz, S. (1983) 'Behavior problems of children as perceived by teachers, mental health professionals, and children.' *Psychology in the Schools 20*, 93–98.

Wilkinson, G.S. (1993) *Wide Range Achievement Test manual* (3rd edition). Wilmington, DE: Wide Range.

Winzer, M. (1999) *Children with Exceptionalities in Canadian Classrooms* (5th edition). Scarborough, Ontario: Prentice Hall Allyn & Bacon Canada.

CHAPTER 8

Students with SEBD as Peer Helpers

Claire Beaumont

INTRODUCTION

Students presenting social, emotional and behaviour problems (SEBD) are now starting to attract teachers' attention at a younger age than ever before. Researchers have discovered that lack of social skills can considerably influence children's affective, cognitive and behavioural development. Amongst these, prosocial skills are critical in the development of positive social relationships. This type of behaviour reveals sensitivity towards other people's needs and is often observed in actions directed towards helping another person while expecting no personal gain in return. Prosocial behaviour is also an important indicator of academic success in school and in social adaptation in general. In an observation study with third grade students (9 years old), Caprara *et al.* (2000) have demonstrated that prosocial behaviour was a significant indicator of school achievement five years later.

There is little evidence however, that this strategy has been usefully applied in the case of students with SEBD. Very often finding themselves as the recipients of support, such students can rarely experience how self-actualizing the experience of helping others can be, since this task is more often given to more socially competent peers. Very few researchers have documented the influence of the development of support skills on the psychosocial adaptation of students with SEBD (Beaumont *et al.* 2003). In most studies dealing with peer support systems, we notice that it is the peer helpers themselves who benefit most from this support system (Casella 2000; Corriveau *et al.* 1998). Indeed by virtue of their role, peer helpers develop their communicative and empathy skills, a better sense of responsibility, better personal problem resolution strategies and improved self-esteem. The studies found in the literature however, deal with peer helpers who had been chosen by their friends because they already had good social skills. We know that lack of social skills and an often negative reputation of behaviourally challenged students exclude such students from being chosen to support their peers, both by the adults and the peers themselves (Bonafé-Schmitt 2000). This is why our research team wanted to know if students with SEBD would benefit when given the opportunity to act as peer helpers in school, and how such a role could be used to help improve their social competence. Before describing our research in this area, it will be useful first to define what we mean by social competence and the framework informing our work. While we can find various published works on social competence, there appears to be an agreement on its definition, namely the effectiveness of interactions with others from the perspective of oneself as well as that of others (Krasnor 1997; Segrin 2000). The theoretical model proposed by Felner, Lease and Phillips (1990) offers an interesting systematic conceptualization on which we based this research. Felner and his colleagues suggest four types of competencies or dominant skills that constitute social competence, namely, cognitive skills and abilities, behavioural skills, emotional competencies, and skills related to motivation and expectancy sets. Prosocial skills form part of the second group of skills, namely behaviour skills.

TEN YEARS OF RESEARCH

For the past ten years our research team has been carrying out studies on peer support systems in special schools for students with severe behaviour difficulties (Beaumont *et al.* 2003; 2004; 2005). The first study took place in a special primary school for students aged 9 to 12. An adapted version of the peer mediation programme *Vers le Pacifique* (Centre Mariebourg 1998a, 1998b) was introduced and evaluated after one scholastic year. Ten workshops dealing with themes related to social skills, conflict resolution and peer mediation were presented to all the students. Once these workshops were completed, 15 mediators were selected by their peers. They participated in additional training in communication skills and interpersonal conflict resolution. Moreover, every month the mediators took part in group supervision meetings and were provided with the services of the progamme's psychologist when needed. During the scholastic year, the mediators were on duty in the school yard following the schedule they had established with their supervisor. They had to wear their identification vest and were responsible for offering their services as mediators when asked to by their peers. A total of 134 mediation sessions were carried out during the scholastic year, and none of the mediators collected disciplinary tickets when on duty. When we evaluated the results of these interventions, it appeared that acting as a peer mediator had a positive influence on the mediator's behavioural self-control, expression of emotions, self-esteem and aggression management (Beaumont *et al*. 2005). Furthermore, a high level of personal satisfaction was expressed by the mediators. Being asked to perform mediation, belonging to a particular team, and being supported by parents and adults at school, were also causes of great satisfaction for these mediators. The self-actualization aspect of this support work was expressed by the helpers themselves as well as by their parents and adults at the school. The teachers expressed their surprise over how children with behaviour difficulties were able to help one another effectively in an environment where previously peer support had not been seen as valuable (Beaumont *et al*. 2005).

Another study (Beaumont, Paquet and Küpfer 2006) was carried in a special high school for students with SEBD. Ten out of the 90 students at the school were selected and trained to act as peer helpers. The process of selecting, training and supervising the helpers was facilitated and monitored by the resident team of school psychologists. The peer helpers formed part of a Student Counselling Service. To consult a student counsellor, students could contact the counsellor directly or else request the service through a school psychologist. A meeting was then held to start the helping process. The student counsellors participated in team supervision meetings twice a month and were provided support by their supervisors on an individual basis when needed. Between January and May, 33 individual interviews were held by the student counsellors, who opined that their work contributed to reducing the level of violence at the school and that it helped many peers to solve personal problems. They also expressed their personal satisfaction at being asked to help fellow students, at being considered worthy of trust by both peers and adults, and at being shown appreciation by parents and staff. The parents of the helpers remarked how proud their children were to participate in this activity, and how this exercise helped to improve their children's listening and communication skills, boost their self-esteem, enhance their sense of responsibility, and promote a greater sense of autonomy.

These studies have demonstrated that despite their behaviour problems, primary and secondary school students were able to develop their social skills when trained in, and encouraged to practise, peer support. Clearly, children and young people with SEBD who act as peer helpers become better skilled in social competence, leading to an improvement in their social interactions.

In the next study we tried to find out which particular social skills were developed when these students practised peer support. The following sections describe this study in more detail.

METHODOLOGY

To analyze the life experience of young persons with SEBD who acted as peer helpers, we adapted and implemented a peer helping programme in a special secondary school. The programme was developed from a British model (Mental Health Foundation 2002) and was aimed at providing additional support to students with personal problems, such as victims of intimidation, or those with depression or relationship problems, who found it difficult to accept professional help. Peer counselling was considered more appropriate in such cases as it allowed a more confidential rapport to be developed between the helper and the one needing help (Beaumont *et al.* 2005).

Data collection was carried out with six students who acted as student counsellors at a special secondary school. These were five boys and one girl, aged between 14 and 16, five of whom had been practising peer helping for the past two years. The six students were all identified as having serious behaviour difficulties which had prevented them from continuing to attend mainstream school. They were elected by their peers to become helpers and participated in a number of training sessions in peer counselling. Finally, they were assisted and supervised by a team of psychologists during the scholastic year.

The participants' experience as student counsellors was analyzed by means of the data collected during semi-structured interviews. The interviews sought the participants' perceptions and experience of peer helping, and its contribution to their personal and social development. Content analysis of the data was carried out through a category-specific system composed of categories emergent from the interview data and other existent conceptual context outcomes. This category-specific system was structured around the four thematic principles proposed by Felner *et al.*'s (1990) typology, namely the participants' emotional competencies, cognitive skills and abilities, behavioural skills, and motivational and expectancy sets. Figure 8.1 shows the thematic organization that guided the analysis. This category-specific system was validated by experts in the field who were able to validate the content according to the chosen conceptual context. The internal consistency was ensured through the verbatim double coding of one part of the data at two different times (Huberman and Miles 1991). The verbatim contents were subsequently coded by means of a computerized qualitative application programme (NVIVO).

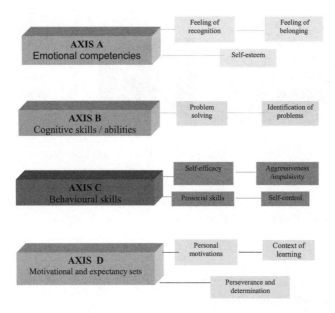

**Figure 8.1: Thematic organization of data from student counsellors at a
special secondary school**

RESULTS

The theoretical model used to describe social competence in the study seems to
correspond well with the findings, since all the participants mentioned each of
the four areas of social competence proposed by Felner *et al.* (1990), namely (in
order of importance) cognitive skills, behavioural skills, emotional skills and
motivational skills. The opinions reported by the participants seem to correspond to the theoretical model used in this study (Felner *et al.* 1990) because
each of the four social skills domains were named during the interview.

Cognitive skills and abilities

As shown in Figure 8.2, the analysis of the young persons' comments reveals
that cognitive skills and abilities are the skills most utilized when students with
SEBD act as peer helpers (49% of the text units revealed and voiced by all peer
helpers). Amongst others, the helpers referred to the use of problem-solving
strategies, the ability to analyze life experience by their clients, the expression

Figure 8.2: Aspects of social competence utilized by students with SEBD when acting as peer helpers

and identification of emotion by the helpers themselves, and the development of moral conscientiousness.

Behavioural skills

Behavioural skills are the set of skills most often reported by the helpers following cognitive skills. Three main behavioural skills emerge from the comments given by the participants, namely the development of empathy, self-efficacy and self-control. Comments about empathy and the self-efficacy were expressed by all the participants at different times but only half the group referred to self-control.

Emotional competencies

All the participants referred to the importance of peer recognition, four out of the six mentioned parental recognition, while three of them underlined the social acceptance by peers. Other comments referred to such aspects as leadership and recognition by adults in the school.

Motivational and expectancy sets

All the peer helpers referred to personal motivation as the main force behind their becoming peer helpers and as maintaining their desire to help their peers. Frequent comments were made by most of the participants about the learning context (motivation to go to school and to see peers solving their problems in the long run) and perseverance and determination (related to the satisfaction experienced at being peer helpers).

Finally, the analysis show that nine distinctive aspects related to social competence could be developed by the students who practised peer support. These aspects were present in all the comments made by the participants, namely recognition by peers, awareness of responsibilities, self-actualization, personal motivation, the development of empathy, the expression of feelings, the identification of problem-solving strategies, self-efficacy and sense of belonging.

DISCUSSION

In line with the previously described studies, the present study lends support to the use of peer helpers in the promotion of social skills amongst students with SEBD attending special schools. Indeed, our studies in primary and secondary special schools demonstrated the relevance and the popularity of this approach in particular school environments. In the light of similar studies conducted with peer helpers not presenting anti-social behaviour, our work also demonstrated the positive impact the practice of peer support has on the social competence skills of students with SEBD. In addition to the validation of Felner *et al.*'s (1990) theoretical model and the contribution of other researchers interested in the development of social competence in young persons, this study provided a better understanding of the motivation underlying young persons as practising peer helpers and threw light on what helps to improve certain aspects of their behaviour (self-control, aggressiveness, self-esteem, expression of emotions, self-efficacy). Thus, peer recognition remains the most important aspect for these young helpers as it gives them an opportunity to be respected and valued for their skills and strengths. It enables them to learn how to recognize their own capacities and develop a feeling of self-efficacy. Indeed, we know that self-esteem is developed from a set of perceptions children have of themselves in different aspects of their lives, their relationships with parents and friends, their academic and athletic life, and perceptions of their own honesty or reliability (Ayotte 2004).

Furthermore, self-esteem lies in the development of essential diverse facets of social competence, such as the sense of belonging (Reasoner 1982). A child is a social being who needs to communicate with others, and the emotional responses he or she receives will influence his or her social behaviour (Bandura 1986). This need to belong to a group is thus very present in a young person, helping him or her to develop his or her own personal identity while affirming his or her similarities to others. The sense of belonging, whether to the group of peer helpers or to a group of students at school, appeared to be present in many of the statements made by the participants in this study. Being engaged in peer support enables the students to learn about collaboration with their peers, a necessary collaboration to satisfy the need to belong (Ayotte 2004). Indeed, by having an acknowledged social role, the young person feels reassured as to the place he or she is given within a group of friends, consequently gaining recognition by virtue of this role.

For peer helpers, the social group becomes a source of positive interactions, creating a feeling of being unique and appreciated. We know that motivation is developed by the reactions produced by our behaviour towards others and the satisfaction we gain from them. Consequently, the perceived positive behaviours on the part of the teachers, the peers and the parents seem to reinforce the young person's desire to practise peer support. The satisfaction of having helped a friend and the acknowledged appreciation of the client impact the helper's desire to pursue his or her role, even in times when motivation is at its weakest. The helpers met various obstacles in the exercise of their duties, such as feeling powerless in given situations, having other activities while on duty, or the refusal of some clients to collaborate. It appears, however, that this perseverance to practise peer support gave them the strength to remain attached to their role. Four of the six peer helpers retained their role till the end of the scholastic year, but two had to leave for family reasons. This finding resonates with other studies with primary school students where the mediators completed the whole year as planned.

Cognitive skills are the most in demand by peer helpers, particularly when they have to listen and analyze reported situations by their 'clients', when they have to reformulate these feelings, or when they have to propose possible solutions to problems. The use of these cognitive activities leads us to believe that when exercising the role of a helper, students will connect to some of their own behaviours when they hear them being formulated by the students they are helping. Indeed, when faced with the same kind of problem met during the helping sessions, the helper is forced to step back and to be able to accompany his or her client in the search of constructive solutions. Having to concentrate on the behaviour of others and assume responsibility as a peacemaker can hardly be compatible with the helper's own inappropriate behaviours. It is paradoxical for the mediator to become angry while he or she is urging clients to stay calm in order to solve their conflict. The student helpers can experience the same emotions as their clients but they have to control themselves. This is illustrated by one student counsellor's comments concerning his own obligation to control himself given the expectations of others towards him. By reformulating in writing, after each consultation, the reported problem situations by the clients and associating to them the feelings expressed, the student counsellors can develop a better emotional vocabulary as well as a larger capacity to understand and relate to situations they themselves could be confronted with.

CONCLUSION

Our research demonstrates that it is beneficial to allow students with SEBD to practise peer support. Previous research has already demonstrated the positive effects on the adaptive behaviour of these students when acting as peer helpers, including expression of emotions, self-esteem, aggression management, behavioural self-control and self-efficacy. The present study has shed light on the type of cognitive, emotional, behavioural and motivational skills developed by peer helpers with SEBD. Peer recognition, responsibility, self-actualization, personal motivation, development of empathy, expression of feelings, identification of problem-solving strategies, self-efficacy, and sense of belonging are the nine aspects which our young peer helpers referred to the most in the interviews. The results support our first hypothesis that the practice of peer support can improve the social competence of young persons with SEBD.

When introducing peer support systems for young persons with SEBD, either in primary or secondary schools, schools have to take into account certain conditions for success that are linked to this type of intervention. Thus, in the eyes of the peer helpers, the teachers' and parents' support is extremely important. Adult guidance is critical to the success of the programme, since these young persons have accumulated many negative experiences in their social interactions. Therefore, it is important to provide regular and adequate supervision, which enables the expression of feelings of helplessness, rejection or incompetence the helpers might have to deal with. Without the adults' support, they risk having to experience an additional social failure with the consequent sense of frustration resulting in a marked increase in SEBD.

REFERENCES

Ayotte, V. (2004) 'Texte sur l'estime de soi.' In *Agir en couleur pour une école en santé*. Québec: Gouvernement du Québec, 2.

Bandura, A. (1986) 'Social Cognitive Theory.' In R. Vasta (ed.) *Annals of Child Development, Vol. 6.* Greenwich: JAI Press.

Beaumont, C., Royer, E., Bertrand, R. and Bowen, F. (2004) 'L'adaptation psychosociale des élèves en trouble de comportement agissant comme médiateurs.' *Revue des Sciences de l'Éducation 30*, 3, 555–579.

Beaumont, C., Royer E., Bertrand, R. and Bowen, F. (2005) 'Les effets d'un programme de médiation par les pairs adapté aux élèves en trouble de comportement.' *Revue Canadienne des Sciences du Comportement 37*, 3, 198–210.

Beaumont, C., Royer E., Bower, F. and Bertrand, R. (2003) 'La médiation par les pairs et les élèves en trouble de comportement.' *Revue de Psychoéducation 32*, 1, 79–103.

Beaumont, C., Paquet, A. and Küpfer, C. (2006) *Le développement des habiletés à l'entraide chez des adolescents en difficulté: expérimentation d'un système d'élèves-confidents en milieu scolaire adapté.* Rapport de recherche présenté au Ministère de l'Éducation, du Loisir et du Sport (MELS); Programme de soutien à la recherche et au développement en adaptation scolaire.

Bonafé-Schmitt, J.P. (2000) *La médiation scolaire par les élèves.* Issy-les-Moulineaux, France: ESF.

Caprara, G.V., Barbaranelli, Pastorelli, C., Bandura, A. and Zimbardo, P.G. (2000) 'Prosocial foundations of children's academic achievement.' *Psychological Science 11*, 302–306.

Casella, R. (2000) 'The benefits of peer mediation in the context of urban conflict and program status.' *Urban Education 35*, 3, 324–355.

Centre Mariebourg (1998a) *La résolution de conflits au primaire: Guide d'animation, Programme Vers le pacifique.* Montreal, Chenelière/McGraw-Hill.

Centre Mariebourg (1998b) *La médiation par les pairs au primaire: Guide d'animation, Programme Vers le pacifique.* Montreal, Chenelière/McGraw-Hill.

Corriveau, D., Bowen, F., Rondeau, N. and Bélanger, J. (1998) 'Faits et questionnements sur l'adaptation psychosociale des enfants médiateurs: Une étude préliminaire.' *Science et Comportement 26*, 3, 171–180.

Felner, R.D., Lease, A.M. and Phillips, R.S.C. (1990) 'Social Competence and the Language of Adequacy as a Subject Matter for Psychology: A Quadripartite Tri-level Framework.' In T.P. Gullotta, G.R. Adams and R. Montemayor (eds) *The Development of Social Competence in Adolescence.* Beverly Hills, CA: Sage.

Huberman, M. and Miles, M.B. (1991) *Analyse des données qualitatives: recueil de nouvelles méthodes.* Brussels: De Boeck University.

Krasnor, L. (1997) 'The nature of social competence: A theoretical review.' *Social Development 6*, 111–135.

Mental Health Foundation (2002) *Peer Support Someone to Turn To.* Evaluation report for the Mental Health Foundation Peer Support Program. London: Mental Health Foundation.

Reasoner, R. (1982) *Building Self-esteem: Elementary Education.* Palo Alto, CA: Consulting Psychologists Press.

Segrin, C. (2000) 'Social skills deficits associated with depression.' *Clinical Psychology Review 20*, 379–403.

CHAPTER 9

Circle Time and Socio-emotional Competence in Children and Young People

Jenny Mosley

INTRODUCTION

'Socio-emotional competence' is a complex term relating to various emotional literacy and social skills. Our preferred definition for 'socio-emotional effectiveness' describes the skills associated with socio-emotional competence as follows:

> A combination of emotional intellect, social effectiveness, and, perhaps, emotional intelligence itself might be represented by the term socio-emotional effectiveness – 'an individual's capacity to navigate the social world in an effective manner, accomplishing his or her goals as needed'. (Mayer and Ciarrochi 2006, p.265)

It is now widely acknowledged that, in order to succeed at school and beyond, not only do children need to become academic learners, but also their whole-person development depends upon their abilities to deal flexibly with personal and interpersonal challenges. In one recent study, three secondary schools who had made promising developments in emotional literacy also reported improvements in areas like learning, academic standards, attendance, behaviour, relationships and improved staff well-being and retention (Lee 2006). In a recent review of studies on socio-emotional competence, the development of children's social, emotional and behavioural skills have been linked to greater educational success, improvements in behaviour, increased inclusion, improved learning, greater social cohesion, and improvements in mental health (Weare and Gray 2003).

CIRCLE TIME

Due to the early pioneering work of a passionate few, circle time is now a commonly used approach, across UK primary schools in particular, for children to practise social and emotional competencies. Though the idea of holding meetings in community circles is almost as old as civilisation itself, in more recent times there have been several pioneers in the field. Ballard and Zimmerman from the USA expanded the idea of circle time in the 1970s and 1980s. White (1999), an exponent on self-esteem and circle time, is well-published in this area, while Robinson and Maines have published various books on areas of emotional literacy including circle time (Bliss, Robinson and Maines 1995; Robinson and Maines 1998).

Circle time is a child-friendly approach encouraging the practice of socio-emotional skills in an inclusive, caring and democratic climate. A variable number of individuals can participate in a circle, which helps everyone to be of equal status and encourages all to participate. It lends itself efficiently to practising skills such as speaking, listening, turn-taking, problem-solving, and enjoying and appreciating each other's company. Some of these skills are key elements of socio-emotional effectiveness. By planning structured and appropriate circle time sessions within a safe and supportive setting, children can participate in stage-appropriate tasks, games and discussions to help develop their self-esteem, self-confidence, emotional literacy and social skills, thereby impacting upon their overall level of socio-emotional competence.

The support given by timetabled weekly circle time sessions and other traditional classroom management systems is sufficient to gain a positive response from the majority of children. For children who are not able readily to access these systems, and whose behaviour is challenging or of concern in some other way, small, focused groupwork sessions are sometimes made available. There are a number of examples of these systems in classrooms today, together with a long history of support groups focusing on anger management, self-esteem and many other areas. Nurture groups (Bennathan and Boxall 1998) are an effective small-group intervention, providing a place and time within school for children to grow socially and emotionally. Usually taking place for part of the school day and in a separate and homely space, groups of up to 12 children undertake an enjoyable and nurturing programme of activities assisted by two adults.

The 'circle of friends' approach (Newton and Wilson 1999; Taylor 1996, 1997) offers a structured intervention based on the belief that a person's judgements about their behaviour and that of others can be influenced by the social situation. The intervention uses small-group sessions to give one specific child positive attention to help them interpret and respond to their environment and social situations with understanding.

The theoretical underpinnings for the many and varied traditional circle time sessions and small-group approaches are far-reaching and may well cite links to a person-centred counselling approach (Mead 1934; Rogers 1961, 1970); social learning theory (Bandura 1977); the circle of friends intervention approach (Newton and Wilson 1999; Taylor 1996, 1997); emotional literacy programmes (Morris and Casey 2005; Morris and Morris 2002); behavioural approaches (Cooper, Smith and Upton 1994); and the eco-systemic approach (Mosley 1993, 1996, 1998). This chapter focuses on two approaches I have developed to promote socio-emotional competencies amongst children, namely Quality Circle Time and the smaller circles of support, and the following sections describe how these two approaches may be used in schools for the promotion of healthy social and emotional development in children.

QUALITY CIRCLE TIME AND CIRCLES OF SUPPORT

Inspired particularly by the groupwork and social dynamics theories of researchers such as Moreno (1934, 1946), Mead (1934), Rogers (1951, 1961), Glasser (1990) and Burns (1979, 1982), I have been developing my own Quality Circle Time model over the last 20 years, and have widely published on all aspects of this circle time model (Mosley 1988, 1989, 1993, 1996, 1998, 2006; Mosley and Tew 1998a, 1998b). Quality Circle Time (QCT) is a generic term for my ecosystemic model, alternatively called the Whole School Quality Circle Time model (see Figure 9.1). The model refers to a whole range of strategies throughout the school that impact positively children's self-esteem and behaviour. It is theoretically underpinned by the approaches listed under the traditional circle time and circles of support approaches described above, and it promotes two types of circle time sessions, namely the mainstream QCT sessions (Mosley 1996, 1998) and circles of support for children with additional emotional or behavioural needs (Mosley and Niwano 2007b).

QCT sessions are a resource for the whole class. They are dynamic and focused sessions that follow a carefully structured five-step model on a regular weekly basis. The sessions are built around the five skills of listening, speaking,

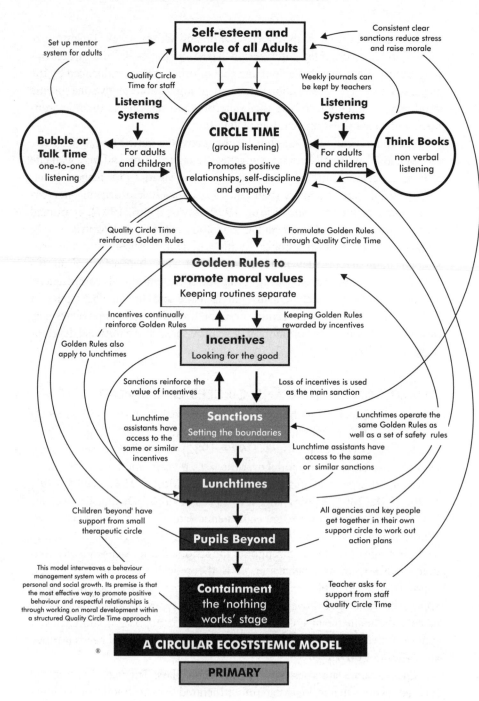

Figure 9.1: The Whole School Quality Circle Time model

looking, thinking and concentrating. On the other hand, circles of support within the QCT model are a smaller, short-term, carefully planned and specifically structured intervention for small groups of children who find it difficult to access class QCT systems and to adhere to agreed behavioural guidelines. Whilst some children (and adults) possess or develop relationship skills naturally, it is possible to teach them to everyone to some degree. Self-esteem theory teaches us that if a person is treated with respect and warmth, 'the individual will see himself as having the characteristics and values that others attribute to him' (Rogers 1961). QCT sessions provide an ideal opportunity for all our intelligences to be stretched and challenged. Children are not only specifically taught the skills they need for personal and social development, but they also learn self-awareness and how to recognise and monitor their own feelings. In addition, they are taught strategies to handle their and others' feelings in a respectful and sensitive way. QCT places great importance on the need for empathy, for understanding another's world, and helps the children to explore and discover successful ways of interacting with others.

Both QCT sessions and circles of support have been used in hundreds of schools for many years in the UK and other countries. In 2005 the Department for Education and Skills (DfES) in England released the *Social and Emotional Aspects of Learning* (SEAL) toolkit for schools (DfES 2005), highlighting the QCT model as a highly effective approach for the delivery of SEAL in schools:

> Circle time is likely to be most effective when embedded within a whole-school approach, such as the Whole School Quality Circle Time model developed by Jenny Mosley. This describes a democratic and practical school management system which addresses social, emotional and behavioural issues through a systemic approach. Its features reflect closely the philosophy, guidance and practice embodied in the SEAL curriculum resource. This model helps schools create the ethos advocated in the resource, by supporting them to create an environment in which social, emotional and behavioural skills can be developed. (DfES 2005, p.54)

Organising a Quality Circle Time session

QCT sessions are designed to provide a safe and effective vehicle for increasing children's communication skills, developing their socio-emotional competences and providing a forum for the class to discuss salient issues. The flexibility of circle time means that the session can also be used to enhance the teaching of language skills and other academic subjects. The sessions are always designed with the following in mind:

- *Structure* – sessions are a timetabled, weekly activity with a five-step plan. Each stage has a specific structure and leads into the next step (see below).

- *Solution-focused* – the atmosphere of safety is reinforced by the requirements of preventing put-downs and negative attitudes, teaching positive behaviours and attitudes, and raising self-esteem.

- *Variety* – a wide range of teaching strategies is available to circle time practitioners, including directed discussion, teaching of thinking and problem-solving skills, and other active methods. Children know that every circle time meeting is different.

QCT meetings progress through five distinct steps, each having a particular purpose. The theme of the meeting will be apparent in each step but will be handled differently at each stage.

1. *Meeting up – playing a game.* Sessions begin with an enjoyable game to help children relax, release tension and feel the joy of being in a group. Games often involve mixing the children up, providing opportunities for new friendships, creating a supportive atmosphere.

2. *Warming up – breaking the silence.* Many children need to 'warm up' to speaking and this is achieved through a speaking and listening 'round' made as straightforward as possible, reducing threat or embarrassment. The teacher introduces a sentence stem, such as 'My favourite animal is…' The facilitator passes a 'speaking object' to the child next to them who repeats the stem, adding their favourite animal, and so on. Any child who does not want to speak may say 'Pass' and pass the object on.

3. *Opening up – exploring issues.* This step is more challenging, an opportunity for important issues to be discussed, such as exploring problems, concerns, hopes and fears, encouraging children to develop a belief in their ability to make responsible choices and decisions. Raising their hands to take turns, children practise specific skills, such as listening or speaking in turn and problem-solving. Children can be encouraged to ask the group for help with something. Members can suggest 'Would it help if…?' Also, Step 3 utilises 'metaphor' through stories, role play, puppets and drama. Through metaphor children can open up about their feelings without having the spotlight put on them.

4. *Cheering up – celebrating the positive.* It can be difficult to 'switch off' from issues of concern, so it is important that children are provided with closing activities that ensure everyone leaves the meeting feeling calm and refreshed. This step celebrates the group's successes and strengths and gives children the opportunity to praise one another or cheer everyone up by giving individual children the chance to teach everyone new skills and games to help everyone feel more competent, happy and positive.

5. *Calming down – bridging.* This is to 'bridge' the session to make a calm transition to the next activity. It may involve a calm game, a song or a guided visualisation. The children learn through this that they can have quiet times safely and calm down, even when they are in a group.

Guidelines are introduced gradually throughout the circle time sessions which are then negotiated and agreed by the children and adults. However the key ground-rule, from the outset, is that no person may mention another in a negative way. They need to say 'Someone is calling me nasty names... Some people are ganging up on me...' Consequently, children learn to stick to the issue and refrain from becoming too personal. A further one-to-one listening system is advocated in schools where children have access to listening so that they can speak openly to a responsible adult about personal issues. It is useful to discuss with the children what should happen if someone breaks a rule and what incentives can be used for keeping the rules.

Organising a QCT circle of support session

Many aspects of running circles of support are similar to class circle time, but the former consist of four to six children who need further support 'beyond' the usual support systems (Mosley and Niwano 2007b). The children chosen will be those finding it difficult to access the main class systems of support and behaviour management. Up to another four children are chosen to join the circle, children who could benefit from attending and who have good social skills. Two facilitators run the sessions so that they can plan activities, liaise with all concerned and share the running of the sessions. Regular reviews take place between the facilitators, children and class teachers to discuss progress. Sessions last from 45 minutes to one hour, although shorter sessions may be used at first. A series of sessions usually lasts a term, although some children may need a longer programme. At the end of the programme, children are care-fully 'bridged' back into the mainstream circle time, accompanied by one of the facilitators during circle time to facilitate the transition from one programme to the other. If children are not seen to be improving, professional support will be sought.

Some practitioners feel the outcomes of circle time and circles of support are difficult to measure, but others choose to use a measurement tool to assess their work. Teachers can use forms of formative assessment, including various 'I can' statements completed by children, and allowing them to assess themselves against these in order to celebrate successes and identify the next targets. In seeking to establish more objective evaluation of outcomes, practitioners may make use of checklists, tests and other standardised measures of socio-emotional competence at pre- and post-interventions.

RESEARCH EVIDENCE

Measuring the qualities associated with socio-emotional effectiveness is complex, with socio-emotional benefits often being subtle, 'soft' and difficult to quantify. Much early research on the effects of QCT programmes was not robust enough for rigorous scientific examination, although the results of such programmes can be seen in action now as schools are openly functioning effectively with these systems in place. The following section discusses various studies on the impact of QCT and circles on socio-emotional competence amongst children and young persons. Some of the research referred to has been published in peer-reviewed journals, while some are taken from unpublished dissertations and reports.

In a survey on the use of circle time in primary schools in Wiltshire and Swindon by Dawson and McNess (1997), 88 per cent of the headteachers stated that they used circle time in their schools, 71 per cent said that it raises self-esteem, 79 per cent said that it increases social skills, 85 per cent stated that it improves communication, and 69 per cent stated that it helps children to take responsibility for their own actions. In another study with primary schools in the UK, Tew (1999) reported that headteachers identified circle time as a powerful system for improving the school ethos, raising self-esteem and promoting the spiritual, cultural, moral, social and personal development of children. Early results from the circle time research by the 'Campaign for Learning' showed that circle time programmes benefited children in many ways, including having more time to reflect up on their feelings, increased readiness to learn, improved resilience and less inappropriate behaviour (Higgins, Wall, Baumfield et al. 2006; Higgins, Wall, Falzon et al. 2005). And results from another study on early-years pupils showed that, alongside an approach to classroom organisation promoting active independent learning, a classroom management approach that centres upon circle time significantly contributes to the personal, social and health education early learning goals (Wood 2001).

In a study on the use of circle time in secondary school (Tew 1998), a difference was found between two Year 7 groups, one being taught PSE (personal and social education) within circle time sessions and the other taught PSE in a normal class setting. After a series of PSE sessions, the circle time group was more familiar with personal information about pupils in the group and was easily able to make positive comments about other people in their group. Teachers involved in the programme at the school also made positive comments relating to pupils' self-confidence, attitude and learning about each other.

In a current large-scale, but still unpublished, study in 16 primary schools in Dublin, Ireland, over three hundred mixed primary-age children completed an evaluation of their experience of circle time. This is an interesting study giving a voice to what the students themselves had to say about their own experience of this approach. The evaluations have been qualitatively examined and the students' responses have been grouped into a number of broad categories, most of which are specific to socio-emotional literacy (Mosley and Niwano 2007a).

- Promotes motivation

    'I love it, absolutely love it.'

    'Feel good because circle time is all about listening, and learning, and having fun.'

- Helps concentration

    'I feel great, the circle time helped me listen and concentrate.'

    'By doing concentration in a fun way.'

- Helps with listening to each other

    'The way everybody settles down and listens to each other.'

    'Everyone was very respectful and they listened and we all had a great time.'

- Promotes teamwork

    'I think it helped because we worked together.'

    'It helped the class work together. We learned to co-operate.'

- Promotes communication

    'We were able to talk without shouting at each other.'

    'I really like it when all the class is sitting down, and we're listening to each other. It is very nice.'

- Helps with making new friends, getting to know other people
  'It helps me learn about other people.'
  'I liked talking about how to make good friends and to work harder.'

- Facilitates expression of feelings, to speak out in class
  'It helps you to spread your feelings.'
  'It helped me to get things off my chest.'

- Promotes self-confidence and sense of belonging
  'I think my class has been helped because it's helped to get us to be confident.'
  'It helped us to know that if something has happened we were not the only ones.'

- Encourages good behaviour, being kind and helpful behaviour
  'We learned to help each other and didn't laugh when people made a try.'
  'I don't think there will be any more bullying.'

As early as 1988 (Mosley 1988) the potential of circle-based support programmes (circles of support) was becoming evident, and small group work was explored into the 1990s successfully, using active experiential activities such as role play, improvisation and games to support pupils who were experiencing social, emotional and behavioural difficulties. In 1991, a school establishing peer support groups in response to the Elton Report (1989, a UK government report on 'Discipline in Schools') found they helped Year 9 and 10 pupils with behavioural and adjustment problems (Shaw 1991). Another study saw young women, referred for low levels of self-esteem, perceiving themselves as being more competent and confident as a result of circle work (Morris 1998). Working in a circle of support with eight Year 6 boys with emotional and behavioural disorders, Franks (2001) reported that the boys became more skilled in expressing their emotions, with indications of improvement in their behaviour. Another study found that Year 7 pupils exhibited increased perception of their own social acceptance after ten weeks of circles of support (Liberman 2003). Circles of support were also used successfully in the Compass for Life project in Stirling (Alcorn 2004), where trainers, working with people aged between 14 and 25 years, used a multi-agency approach focusing upon employability through participative learning programmes. After a three-month programme, it was reported that the circle of support had helped the participants understand themselves and others better and to appreciate more what they had to say, and stopped the use of put-downs in their social interactions.

CONCLUSION

Circle time and circles of support are widely used in schools in the UK and abroad by various practitioners. The experiences and opportunities offered during such sessions are designed to support children in developing their social, communication, emotional, problem-solving and learning skills. The evidence suggests that both circle time and circles of support contribute to the social and emotional effectiveness of those taking part in the programmes. Moreover, the many reports from educational practitioners and children themselves, as well as the unending popularity of circle time in schools and other contexts, also suggest that circle time and circles of support are found to be helpful and useful by many in the promotion of social and emotional competences in children and young people. Circle times and circles of support continue to be used successfully by enthusiastic practitioners in many different settings. The indications are that circle time and circles of support work and help to make a difference in the social and emotional development of children and young persons. However, more research is urgently needed to examine the impact of circle time and circles of support more thoroughly, extensively and rigorously and to determine the ways this approach works most effectively for children and young persons' socio-emotional competence.

REFERENCES

Alcorn, J. (2004) *Post-school Learning and Self-esteem: Using Quality Circle Time in the Stirling Compass for Life Partnership*. Trowbridge: Jenny Mosley Consultancies.

Bandura, A. (1977) *Social Learning Theory*. Englewood Cliffs, NJ: Prentice-Hall.

Bennathan, M. and Boxall, M. (1998) *The Boxall Profile: Handbook for Teachers*. London: Nurture Group Network.

Bliss, T., Robinson, G. and Maines, B. (1995) *Developing Circle Time: Taking Circle Time Much Further*. London: Lucky Duck.

Burns, R. (1979) *The Self Concept*. London: Longman.

Burns, R. (1982) *Self Concept Development and Emotion*. London: Holt Saunders.

Cooper, P., Smith, C.J. and Upton, G. (1994) *Emotional and Behavioural Difficulties: Theory to Practice*. London: Routledge.

Dawson, N. and McNess, E. (1997) *A Report on the Use of Circle Time in Wiltshire Primary Schools*. Unpublished report commissioned by Wiltshire Local Education Authority.

Department for Education and Science (DfES) (2005) *Excellence and Enjoyment: Social and Emotional Aspects of Learning (SEAL)*. Nottingham: DFES Publications.

Franks, G. (2001) *Can Circle Time Facilitate the Learning of Emotional Expression and Competence in Boys with Severe EBD?* Unpublished MEd thesis, School of Education, University of Bristol.

Glasser, W. (1990) *Reality Therapy*. New York: Harpers and Collins.

Higgins, S., Wall, K., Baumfield, V., Hall, E., Leat, D. and Woolner, P. with Clark, J., Edwards, G., Falzon, C., Jones, H., Lofthouse, R., Miller, J., Moseley, D., McCaughey, C. and Mroz, M. (2006) *Learning to Learn in Schools Phase 3 Evaluation: Year Two Report*. London: Campaign for Learning.

Higgins, S., Wall, K., Falzon, C., Hall, E., Leat, D., Baumfield, V., Clark, J., Edwards, G., Jones, H., Lofthouse, R., Moseley, D., Miller, J., Murtagh, L., Smith, F., Smith, H. and Woolner, P. (2005) *Learning to Learn in Schools Phase 3 Evaluation: Year One Final Report*. London: Campaign for Learning.

Lee, K. (2006) *More Than a Feeling: Developing the Emotionally Literate Secondary School.* Nottingham: National College for School Leadership.

Liberman, J. (2003) *Can a Circle of Support Help to Boost the Self-concept, Social Skills and Modify the Behaviour of Pupils in Year 7 at a Secondary School?* Unpublished MEd thesis, School of Education, University of Bristol.

Mayer, J.D. and Ciarrochi, J. (2006) 'Clarifying Concepts Related to Emotional Intelligence: A Proposed Glossary.' In J. Ciarrochi, J. Forgas and J.D. Mayer (eds) *Emotional Intelligence in Everyday Life* (2nd edition). New York: Psychological Press.

Mead, G.H. (1934) *Mind, Self and Society.* Chicago: University of Chicago Press.

Moreno, J.L. (1934) *Who Shall Survive?* New York: Plenum Press.

Moreno, J.L. (1946) *Psychodrama* (2nd revised edition). Ambler, PA: Beacon House.

Morris, A. (1998) *Groupwork with Self Referred Young Women with Low Self-esteem.* Unpublished MEd thesis, School of Education, University of Bristol.

Morris, E. and Casey, J. (2005) *Developing Emotionally Literate Staff: A Practical Guide.* London: Paul Chapman Educational Publishing.

Morris, E. and Morris, K. (2002) *The Powerhouse: An All-in-One Resource for Building Self-Esteem in Primary Schools.* London: Lucky Duck.

Mosley, J. (1988) 'Some implications arising from a small-scale study of a circle-based programme initiated for the tutorial period.' *Pastoral Care,* June, 10–16.

Mosley, J. (1989) *All Round Success.* Trowbridge: Wiltshire Local Education Authority.

Mosley, J. (1993) *Turn Your School Round.* Cambridge: LDA.

Mosley, J. (1996) *Quality Circle Time.* Cambridge: LDA.

Mosley, J. (1998) *More Quality Circle Time.* Cambridge: LDA.

Mosley, J. (2006) *Step-by-Step Guide to Circle Time for SEAL.* Trowbridge: Positive Press.

Mosley, J. and Tew, M. (1998a) *Important Issues Relating to the Promotion of Positive Behaviour in Secondary Schools.* Trowbridge: Jenny Mosley Consultancies.

Mosley, J. and Tew, M. (1998b) *Quality Circle Time in the Secondary School: A Handbook of Good Practice.* London: David Fulton.

Mosley, J. and Niwano, Z. (2007a) *An Informal Report on the Use of Jenny Mosley's Whole School Quality Circle Time Model in Dublin Primary Schools.* Unpublished.

Mosley, J. and Niwano, Z. (2007b) *They're Driving me Mad: Running Circles of Support for Children Whose Behaviour Pushes You Beyond Your Limit.* Cambridge: LDA.

Newton, C. and Wilson, D. (1999) *Circles of Friends.* Dunstable and Dublin: Folens.

Robinson, G. and Maines, B. (1998) *Circle Time Resources.* London: Chapman & Hall.

Rogers, C. (1951) *Client Centered Therapy.* Boston, MA: Houghton Mifflin.

Rogers, C. (1961) *On Becoming a Person: A Therapist's View of Psychotherapy.* Boston, MA: Houghton Mifflin.

Rogers, C. (1970) *Carl Rogers on Encounter Groups.* New York: Harper and Row.

Shaw, K. (1991) 'Setting up peer support groups: one school's INSET response to the Elton Report.' *Pastoral Care,* December, 13.

Taylor, G. (1996) 'Creating a circle of friends: A Case Study.' In H. Cowie and S. Sharp (eds) *Peer Counselling in School.* London: David Fulton.

Taylor, G. (1997) 'Community building in schools: Developing a circle of friends.' *Educational and Child Psychology 14,* 45–50.

Tew, M. (1998) 'Circle time: A much-neglected resource in secondary schools?' *Pastoral Care,* September, 24–26.

Tew, M. (1999) *A Report on the Use of Jenny Mosley's Whole School Quality Circle Time Model in Primary Schools in the U.K.* Commissioned by All Round Success. Unpublished.

Weare, K. and Gray, G. (2003) *What Works in Developing Children's Emotional and Social Competence and Well-being?* DfES Research Report 456. Southampton: The Health Education Unit, Research and Graduate School of Education.

White, M. (1999) *Magic Circles: Building Self-esteem Through Circle Time.* London: Lucky Duck.

Wood, F. (2001) *Can Circle Time in the Foundation Stage Support the Early Learning Goals for Personal, Social and Emotional Development?* Unpublished dissertation, School of Education, University of Bristol.

PART 3

Working with Students' Emotions

CHAPTER 10

Nurture Groups: An Evaluation of the Evidence

Paul Cooper

INTRODUCTION

Nurture groups are small classes in infant, primary and secondary schools for students with social, emotional, behavioural and learning problems.

A classic nurture group reflects the following principles (Bennathan and Boxall 2000):

- They are located on the site of a mainstream primary or infant school, but can be located in a secondary school.

- They cater for 10–12 children who are already on the roll of the host school.

- They are staffed by two adults: a teacher and a full-time teaching assistant.

- They operate for nine out of ten half-day sessions in the school week.

- Nurture group pupils remain on the roll of a mainstream class; register with this class daily, and spend curriculum time in this class when not attending the nurture group.

- Full-time placement in a mainstream class is the main object of nurture group placement.

- The nurture group provides a holistic curriculum, incorporating the UK National Curriculum with a curriculum designed to address social, emotional and behavioural factors underpinning academic learning.

A central aim of nurture groups is therefore to provide students with a secure and safe environment that provides the conditions necessary for them to develop emotionally, socially and cognitively (Boxall 2002). In classic nurture groups, the lessons are highly structured and the nurture group staff ensure a slow-moving and routinised learning environment, within which pupils' experiences are carefully managed.

Nurture groups are temporary separated transitional settings that prepares students to cope better with the demands of mainstream schooling. Nurture group candidates often present social, emotional and behavioural difficulties that prevent them (and sometimes their peers) from engaging with the schooling experience constructively. Nurture groups are specifically designed to remove or reduce these barriers and, therefore, prevent these children from disengaging with the education system, ideally in the early stages of their educational history. In addition, nurture groups can have profound and positive effects on whole schools, as well as on relationships within families, such as between parents and children or between siblings (Cooper and Whitebread 2007).

THE DEVELOPMENT OF NURTURE GROUPS

Nurture groups are not a new form of educational provision. They were devised by Marjorie Boxall, an educational psychologist, who set up the first groups in the Inner London Education Authority in the early 1970s (Bennathan and Boxall 2000) in the UK. Having gone through an initial period of popularity, which lasted for the best part of a decade, nurture groups dwindled in numbers, with many of the original groups being closed down (Bennathan and Boxall 2000). In 1998, a national survey found less than 50 groups in the UK (Cooper, Arnold and Boyd 1998). Current (unpublished) evidence identifies over 400 groups throughout the UK. This figure reflects only those groups that have registered with the Nurture Group Network. Even at 400, this represents an 800 per cent increase over five years. Informed estimates, however, suggest that there may well be 1000 NGs in the UK, many of which are not registered with the NGN.

The possible reasons for this dramatic increase in numbers are complex. Over the decade of the 1990s the overall rate of permanent pupil exclusions from school increased by approximately 400 per cent, with the highest rates of increase being found in the primary schools (Castle and Parsons 1998). More recent findings suggest that National Curriculum testing leads to increased stress levels among Year 6 pupils (Connor 2001, 2003). Other evidence suggests that the 1990s is marked by increasing levels of stress and insecurity in schools, reflected in perceptions of rising levels of emotional and behavioural difficulties among pupils and work overload among teachers, leading to severe problems in recruiting and retaining teaching staff in schools (Johnson and Hallgarten 2002). The more recent evidence suggests that wider cultural changes and the growing dominance of individualism in Western culture is a major threat to the social and emotional wellbeing of young people (James 2007, 2008; Layard and Dunn 2009) (see Chapter 14).

STUDENTS IN NURTURE GROUPS
Specific, targeted attention

It is generally believed that the children who will benefit most from nurture groups are those who, for whatever reason, have a need for a classroom set-up that allows more individual attention than is often available in the mainstream classroom. For this reason there are usually between 10 and 12 students in a nurture group, and the group will be staffed by two adults, usually a teacher and a teaching assistant (paid assistants who support pupils in a variety of ways in schools; referred to as 'paraprofessionals' and 'paraeducators' in the US). This means that the students each have many opportunities to speak to adults and to get help with their schoolwork. It also means that the adults get to know each student really well. These factors combine to help the adults and the students work together in ways that enable each student to get access to experiences that will help them develop and improve their learning skills as well as the abilities to understand and manage their feelings and get along with other children.

Some of the children in the nurture group, when they first start attending the group, will be very quiet and withdrawn, whilst others may have a tendency to be excitable and disruptive. Because the members of staff are able to give such close attention to each student, they are able to work hard at getting the quiet students to 'come out of themselves' by engaging them in conversation and designing activities that will gradually help them to feel more comfortable with interacting with other children. They are also able to help students to deal with anger problems, and, by observing children carefully, spot the situations that normally lead to disruptive behaviour for specific students. Staff can then prevent disruption from happening. For example, they can do this by teaching the child specific skills for dealing with problem situations (e.g. how to deal with other pupils wanting to borrow equipment); by distracting students from the negative situations (e.g. engaging pupils in an alternative activity whilst the teacher deals with the request to borrow the equipment), and so on. This is not to say that nurture group staff are always successful in preventing pupils in the nurture group from misbehaving. It would be a very unusual pupil who did not misbehave, sometimes. When pupils in the nurture group misbehave the staff will respond, dealing with the behaviour in ways that are designed to encourage pupils to learn that the best way of getting what they want is to behave in ways that are considerate of other people's feelings.

Links between learning, feelings and behaviour

Obviously, the main purpose of schooling is to promote students' learning. However, it is increasingly apparent that the kind of learning that is supposed to go on in schools is often undermined by feelings of emotional insecurity that prevent students from concentrating and participating with others. In fact, nurture groups are built on the principle that the foundations of learning are emotional and social.

A very important feature of the nurture group approach is an understanding of the ways in which the kinds of learning that children are expected to do in schools is closely linked to how they feel about themselves, and how well they are able to get along with other children. It is argued that learning problems, such as difficulties in learning how to read, or problems with understanding numbers, can sometimes be the result of a child's feelings of fear and anxiety acting as a barrier to the child's engagement with the learning task. This reminds us just how stressful the whole business of learning can be.

Every time a teacher asks a student to try to carry out a learning activity, there is always the possibility that the student will not perform the activity as well as he or she might, or as well as the teacher expects, or as well as other children in the same classroom. We have all been in this situation as children, and we continue to experience similar situations in our adult lives. Although learning new skills can be fun, it can also be very threatening. When we succeed at learning something new it makes us feel good about ourselves. Do you remember when you passed your driving test, or the first time you successfully decorated a room, or when you did anything for the first time that you thought you might not be able to do? Success breeds success. Once you have succeeded in overcoming one challenge, you have a little more confidence the next time you are confronted with a similar challenge.

Students who benefit most from being in nurture groups are those who seem to have particular difficulty in engaging with classroom learning and getting along with other students in their age group, and who become anxious or angry when in learning situations. The nurture group provides a comfortable and caring environment in which opportunities are given to students that allow them to engage in activities according to their particular level of need. This means that children who have had difficulty in learning how to play will be given the chance to engage in play, at first with an adult, and later with other children and on their own. It is through these experiences that students develop the skills necessary to operate in a classroom group.

In order for students to feel confident about play and work it is important that they feel safe and secure. Nurture group staff work hard to encourage these feelings in their students through the ways in which they talk to the children, and by providing activities that help the children develop a sense of belonging to the group. The nurture group room is also specially designed to help students feel comfortable and safe. This is achieved by having all of the features of a normal classroom (e.g. books, desks, whiteboard, computers) along with items that would normally be found in a comfortable home setting (e.g. carpets, soft furnishings, dining table, cooking facilities).

All of these features of the nurture group are directed at helping students feel secure, feel good about themselves, and feel able to work on formal National Curriculum topics and, therefore, make educational progress. In short, the nurture group sets out to help students develop a positive feeling towards school, that is based on: feelings of safety in the school setting; the experience of being cared for by the nurture group staff; the experience of success in getting along with other students, and the experience of achievement in learning activities. All of the time that students are in the nurture group, they are also keeping in close contact with their mainstream class. This prevents nurture group students from developing feelings of exclusion from their mainstream peers. After a relatively short period of time (usually from three to four school terms) they are generally able to return to the mainstream on a full-time basis.

EVIDENCE FROM RESEARCH

In a study by Iszatt and Wasilewska (1997), of 308 children placed in nurture groups between 1984 and 1996, 87 per cent were able to return to the mainstream after a placement duration of less than one year. In 1995 this group was revisited, and it was found that 83 per cent of the original cohort were still in mainstream placements with only 4 per cent requiring special educational needs support beyond the schools' standard ranges of provision. Of the original cohort, 13 per cent were granted Statements of Special Educational Need, and 11 per cent were referred to special school provision. This finding was contrasted with data on a non-matched group of 20 mainstream pupils who had been designated as requiring nurture group placement but for whom places had not been found. Of these, 35 per cent were placed in special schools and only 55 per cent were found, by 1995, to be coping in mainstream classrooms without additional support.

In the absence of adequate matching measures, it is difficult to interpret the significance of differences in outcomes for the two groups. However, the positive performance of the majority of nurture group cohort was consistent with studies of staff perceptions of the effects of nurture group placement assessed in other studies that point to improvements in pupils' self-management behaviours, social skills, self-awareness and confidence, skills for learning and approaches to learning (Boorn 2002; Cooper and Lovey 1999; Doyle 2001). O'Connor and Colwell (2003) assessed the performance of 68 five-year-old children placed in three nurture groups for a mean period of 3.1 terms. They found statistically significant mean improvements in terms of cognitive and emotional development, social engagement and behaviours indicative of secure attachment. Boxall data was also reported on an opportunity sample ($n = 12$) of the original cohort after two years. Findings suggest that many of the improvements had been maintained, though there was evidence of relapse in some areas of emotional and social functioning.

A national longitudinal study over two years (Cooper, Arnold and Boyd 2001) investigated the effectiveness of nurture groups within 25 schools, in eight local education authority areas. In this study, the effectiveness of nurture groups was judged by comparing pupils with two different control groups: one consisting of pupils matched according to age, gender, educational attainment and level of social, emotional and behavioural difficulties (SEBD) in mainstream classrooms; the other of pupils matched for age and gender with the nurture group children but without emotional and behavioural problems. On the basis of variations amongst different nurture groups in the sample, the authors did not report any statistically different outcomes, however positive perceptions towards to nurture groups were noted. In particular, mainstream teacher interviews reported a strong positive impact of nurture groups in terms of children's progress in their educational attainment as well as the development of a 'nurturing' environment in many aspects of school life.

A subsequent comprehensive paper (Cooper and Whitebread 2007) explored the effects of nurture groups over two years on a large cohort of children ($n = 546$), including a significant number of children who were attending nurture groups ($n = 356$). Quantitative evidence was gathered that indicated greater significant improvements for the nurture group children's social, emotional and behavioural functioning. Of particular interest was the fact that students with SEBD who were not placed in nurture groups, but were in mainstream classes in a school housing a nurture group, achieved significantly better outcomes than pupils with SEBD who attended schools that did not have nurture groups. This indicated a significant whole-school effect of the nurture group intervention. This study also suggested that the groups that had been in existence for two years or more were more effective than those that had been in existence for less than two years. This finding was interpreted as indicating the importance of cumulative experience in promoting the effectiveness of the provision.

In line with other studies, the parents of nurture group pupils reported positive perceptions of nurture groups. A further, extremely interesting and unexpected finding was the claim made by some parents that an indirect effect of nurture group placement had been an improvement in the quality of parent–child relationships in the home setting. It should be stressed that this finding was elicited from telephone interviews carried out with fewer than 100 parents/carers. This is a weak method for exploring issues as complex as parent–child relationships. The finding is, however, worthy of further and more rigorous investigation.

Hitherto unpublished findings from this study are also of interest. In particular it was found that there were systematic differences in the generalisation of effects of nurture groups on students presenting with different characteristics. The quantitative evidence from this study suggests that children with a very wide range of social, emotional and behavioural difficulties, showed dramatic improvements in their social and emotional functioning when they are placed in nurture groups. Students who have previous presented with serious conduct problems, peer-related problems, emotional problems and hyperactivity were shown to perform significantly better when they are when placed in nurture groups than matched students who weren't. However, when those same students were observed in mainstream classrooms, those with primarily conduct and social problems appeared to sustain the improvements attributed to nurture group placement, while students whose difficulties were characterised as primarily relating to hyperactivity or emotional symptoms were statistically not likely to generalise the improvements to the mainstream classes. These findings can be interpreted in a number of ways, the most persuasive of which appears to be that serious emotional disturbance and chronic hyperactivity may well have stronger individualised, within-child causes than other SEBDs, making it particularly difficult for individuals with the problems to adapt to the mainstream classroom. An extension to this argument is that if mainstream classrooms are to become capable of including children with such difficulties, then they must do more to target the specific needs of these groups.

Among other smaller-scale studies, those of Bishop and Swain (2000a, 2000b) explored the effectiveness in an inner-city area of severe deprivation of a nurture group consisting of children in Years 1 to 3. The researchers also reported a parent–school partnership model and explained this in consideration of a 'transplant model', which implies that the skills and expertise of teachers are passed to parents through their engagement to the nurture group (Cunningham and Davis 1985; Dale, cited in Bishop and Swain 2000b). Howes, Emanuel and Farrell (2003) question the potential of nurture groups in facilitating inclusive practice. Having reviewed three varying case studies, the authors identified the size of group, the age of children and the mixture of emotional and behavioural difficulties that they exhibit as critical in relation to effective running of the nurture group, they also questioned the opportunity cost of the nurture group, asking what those children lose when they separated from their peer groups in the mainstream settings.

Doyle (2003) reported that setting up a nurture group in her school, however, had the result of spreading nurturing practices into the whole school, a finding consistent with that of Binnie and Allen (2008), and consistent with the whole-school effect of nurture groups identified by Cooper and Whitebread (2007) (see above).

Recently, an important study was carried out with 179 pupils aged between five and seven years with SEBDs attending schools in Glasgow (Reynolds and Kearney 2007). Approximately half of the group were attending nurture groups in 16 schools, and approximately half were attending 16 schools without nurture group provision. It was found that the nurture group pupils had made significant improvements in self-esteem, self-image, emotional maturity and attainment in literacy when compared to the group of pupils attending the schools without nurture group provision. These studies point towards distinctive effects of nurture group placement on pupil progress, and suggest that positive progress in key areas of development targeted by nurture groups takes place during placement in a nurture group.

Questions remain about the extent to which the nurture group approach can be changed and adapted without compromising the effectiveness of the approach. Cooper and Whitebread (2007) found no significant differences between full- and part-time groups. This finding is confirmed in a small-scale study by Scott and Lee (2009).

A WORD OF CAUTION

Whilst it is clearly the case that the existing research evidence on nurture groups is highly positive, there remain some concerns about this form of provision that warn against the dangers of accepting this or any other form of educational intervention uncritically. In interviews with nurture group and mainstream staff, Cooper and Tiknaz (2005) enquired about areas where staff working with effective nurture groups felt there was room for improvement in nurture group provision.

Communication

A particular area of concern was the issue of communication between main-stream and nurture group staff. Nurture group students depend heavily on the quality of this channel of communication to maximise the all important conti-nuity of the educational experience they receive as they move between nurture group and mainstream provision. Both nurture group and mainstream staff spoke of difficulties they encountered when communication was poor. Some interviewees indicated that there may sometimes be an over-reliance on the personalities of the staff to promote communication, suggesting that this aspect of nurture group provision should be programmed into whole-school management of nurture groups.

Opportunity Cost

Some mainstream staff expressed concern about the decline in educational performance that they observed in some children who were placed in nurture groups. This was sometimes expressed in terms of a tendency among some students to exhibit apparent reductions in their levels of motivation when placed among students performing at lower levels than their mainstream classmates. It should be stressed that this is anecdotal and unsupported evidence. However, it reflects a genuine concern that needs to be considered by nurture group and mainstream staff.

Exclusion

Perhaps the single most important challenge that nurture groups face, is the perception that nurture groups may be used as a means of excluding trouble-some students from mainstream classrooms as a social control measure. Evidence from several of the studies reported on already in this chapter tend to challenge this perception forcefully, by indicating that nurture groups both protect students from exclusion from school and have been shown to make a major contribution to promoting the social and educational engagement of students into mainstream classrooms. The crucial point here, of course, is that these positive effects are entirely dependent on the integrity of the provision.

This means that schools that take on nurture groups must ensure that they adhere to the established principles of nurture group provision. The dangers of failing to do this are considerable. After all, a nurture group that does not conform to the principles expounded by Bennathan and Boxall (1998) is not a nurture group at all. As nurture groups become increasingly widespread the danger of such bastardisation becomes increasingly likely.

CONCLUSION

The existing published evidence on the effects of nurture groups is supportive of the intervention. It is important, however, to note that the research base relies on naturalistic studies. One of the advantages of these studies is that they have helped to define the nature of nurture groups. There is still a need, however, for more controlled studies of this form of provision.

REFERENCES

Bennathan, M. and Boxall, M. (1998) *The Boxall Profile: Handbook for Teachers*. London: Nurture Group Network.

Bennathan, M. and Boxall, M. (2000) *Effective Intervention in Primary Schools: Nurture Groups*. London: David Fulton.

Binnie, L.M. and Allen, K. (2008) 'Whole school support for vulnerable children: The evaluation of a part-time nurture group.' *Emotional and Behavioural Difficulties 13*, 3, pp.201–216.

Bishop, A. and Swain, J. (2000a) 'Early years education and children with behavioural and emotional difficulties: Nurturing parental involvement.' *Emotional and Behavioural Difficulties 5*, 4, 26–31.

Bishop, A. and Swain, J. (2000b) 'The bread, the jam and some coffee in the morning: Perceptions of a nurture group.' *Emotional and Behavioural Difficulties 5*, 3, 18–24.

Boorn, C. (2002) *Locating a Nurture Group: Identifying and Evaluating Features within a School that Would Make a Suitable Host*. Unpublished MSc thesis, University of Sheffield.

Boxall, M. (2002) *Nurture Groups in School: Principle and Practice*. London: Paul Chapman.

Castle, F. and Parsons, C. (1998) 'Disruptive behaviour and exclusions from school: Redefining and responding to the problem.' *Emotional and Behavioural Difficulties 2*, 3, 1–15.

Connor, M. (2001) 'Pupil stress and standard assessment tasks.' *Emotional and Behavioural Difficulties 6*, 2, 103–111.

Connor, M. (2003) 'Pupil stress and standard assessment tasks: An update.' *Emotional and Behavioural Difficulties 8*, 2, 101–107.

Cooper, P., Arnold, R. and Boyd, E. (1998) *The Nature and Distribution of Nurture Groups In England and Wales*. Cambridge: University of Cambridge School of Education.

Cooper, P., Arnold, R. and Boyd, E. (2001) *Evaluation of Nurture Group Provision in an English LEA*. Unpublished research report. University of Leicester.

Cooper, P. and Lovey, J. (1999) 'Early intervention in emotional and behavioural difficulties: The role of nurture groups.' *European Journal of Special Needs Education 14*, 2, 122–131.

Cooper, P. and Tiknaz, Y. (2005) 'Progress and challenge in Nurture Groups: Evidence from three case studies.' *British Journal of Special Education 32*, 4, 211–222.

Cooper, P. and Whitebread, D. (2007) 'The effectiveness of nurture groups on student progress: Evidence from a national research study.' *Emotional and Behavioural Difficulties 12*, 3, 171–190.

Cunningham, C.C. and Davis, H. (1985) *Working with Parents: Frameworks for Collaboration*. Buckingham: Open University Press.

Doyle, R. (2001) 'Using a readiness scale for reintegrating pupils with social, emotional and behavioural difficulties from a nurture group into their mainstream classroom: A pilot study.' *British Journal of Special Education 28*, 3, 126–132.

Doyle, R. (2003) 'Developing the nurturing school: Spreading nurture group principles and practices into mainstream classrooms.' *Emotional and Behavioural Difficulties 8*, 4, 253–267.

Howes, A., Emanuel, J. and Farrell, P. (2003) 'Can Nurture Groups Facilitate Inclusive Practice in Primary Schools?' In P. Farrell and M. Ainscow (eds) *Making Special Education Inclusive.* London: David Fulton.

Iszatt, J. and Wasilewska, T. (1997) 'Nurture groups: An early intervention model enabling vulnerable children with emotional and behavioural difficulties to integrate successfully into school.' *Educational and Child Psychology 14*, 3, 121–139.

James, O. (2007) *Affluenza.* London: Vermilion.

James, O. (2008) *The Selfish Capitalist.* London: Vermilion.

Johnson, P. and Hallgarten, R. (2002) *From Victims of Change to Agents of Change: The Future of the Teaching Profession.* London: Policy Studies Institute.

Layard, R. and Dunn, J. (2009) *A Good Childhood.* London: Penguin.

O'Connor, T. and Colwell, J. (2003) 'The effectiveness and rationale of the "nurture group" approach to helping children with emotional and behavioural difficulties remain within mainstream education.' *British Journal of Special Education 29*, 2, 96–100.

Reynolds, S. and Kearney, M. (2007) *Nurture Groups: The Answer to Everything?* Paper presented to the British Psychological Society Education Division Annual Conference.

Scott, K. and Lee, A. (2009) 'Beyond the "classic" nurture group model: An evaluation of part-time and cross age nurture groups in a Scottish local authority.' *Support for Learning 24*, 1, 5–10.

CHAPTER 11

Nurture Groups: Early Relationships and Mental Health

Marion Bennathan

INTRODUCTION

Most of us who work with young people in difficulty, believe that without early effective help they are in danger of ending up with wasted lives, perhaps with mental health problems, perhaps as criminals. This adds urgency to our work, putting it in a different time frame. But what do we know about what really works for such young people? And do people in positions of influence agree with us? This chapter draws on recent developments in neuroscience and pharmacology to throw light on the relationship between early relationships in childhood and mental health in adulthood, underlining the role of nurture groups in providing for healthy early relationships amongst children who may be at risk in their socio-emotional development.

When I was helping to set up Young Minds in the UK in 1991, a colleague and I went to discuss funding with the senior civil servant whose job was to allocate resources for child mental health. He told us that he had just been informing himself about mental health problems by spending time working in a large psychiatric hospital. He had been surprised, reading through the patients' records, to find how many of them had had very unhappy childhoods. He wondered whether there was a connection. We had no hesitation in giving him an answer. In 1996, a question was asked in the British Parliament about the shortage of services for children and young people with mental health problems, and the implication of such shortage for their future. The Minister replied that there was no scientific research that showed a clear connection between childhood problems and adult outcomes. Though we cannot really be precise about this relationship, the current developments in neuroscience and pharmacology have a direct bearing on this question and provide useful insights in our discussion on the connection between early negative relationships and later mental health problems.

WHAT CAN WE LEARN FROM NEUROSCIENCE

In 1953 Watson and Crick published their DNA research, which revealed the bio-chemical basis of life, of brain function, of how genes are transmitted from one generation to the next. This has led to rapid and exciting developments in understanding ever more precisely how our genetic make-up is inherited, to identifying diseases more exactly so that cures become possible. Developments in neuroscience and in appropriate pharmacology are reshaping the understanding of mental health problems and their treatment. We now have the ability to scan the nervous system and understand much better the functioning of the human brain.

There are obvious problems in fundamental research on children, but since we share 98.9 per cent of our genetic make-up with other mammals, Michael Meaney's mice experiments become quite relevant. Professor of Medicine at McGill University in Canada, his interests are in 'early environmental regulation of gene expression'; that is, the way early experience exerts an influence on brain development. Lecturing at an American Psychiatric Association Meeting in Toronto in 2006, Meaney decribed how he took two groups of mice with new born 'pups'. He separated the mothers into the 'good', as measured by the amount of feeding, grooming and nuzzling they gave their babies, and the 'bad' mothers. He measured the brain development of the two groups of pups. Those with good mothers had healthy development, those with bad mothers had poor development. He then switched the babies over. Later measurements showed that the development of the two groups had evened out.

Such research is clearly not possible in humans. But occasionally a situation arises where similar research into child development is possible. The English and Romanian Adoptees Project is a long-running research project under the auspices of Michael Rutter (Rutter *et al.* 2007). Two groups of children adopted by British families were studied, one from conditions of extreme deprivation in Romanian orphanages and the other from stable family backgrounds in England. Not surprisingly, the younger the age at adoption of the Romanian children, the less the difference in development was reported. Rutter and his colleagues reported greater cognitive catching-up than might have been predicted even in Romanian children adopted at an older age. On the other hand, the social development, including that of the early adopted (0–6 months) Romanian children, showed significant deficits. Also a surprisingly high number of children (6%) exhibited autistic or quasi-autistic behavioural patterns at the previous assessments. The suggestion that social deprivation is associated with autistic-like behaviours is particularly interesting because it challenges our current understanding of the disorder. Problems in attention and hyperactivity were also noted in a significant number of children, and this, too, was positively associated with the duration of deprivation.

Schizophrenia is one of the mental health conditions generally considered to have a strong genetic element. At a Royal College of Psychiatry conference in 2005, a young scientist presented a highly scientific and enthusiastic description of the part of the genome that mediates schizophrenia. I listened somewhat dismayed as he seemed to imply that the condition simply unrolled. Just one sentence, his last, indicated that environment might matter: 'Untoward life circumstances may have an influence.' He was immediately followed by Robin Murray, Head of the Institute of Psychiatry in London, who compared the incidence of schizophrenia in young men of Jamaican descent born in London and those brought up in Jamaica. The first was much higher. This links with a telling phrase used by Micheal Meaney in his lecture, 'the nurture of nature'. We have our genes but they are not all-powerful; their development will partly depend on the circumstances of our life. The question then arises for us working with children who may or may not be at risk genetically: How do we provide the nurture that will help them to flourish even if their genes are less than ideal? We know that if early damage is left unaddressed it becomes worse, but a secure, safe and caring upbringing helps them to thrive.

The Nobel Prize-winning biologist Eric Kandel, started his life as a psychiatrist, greatly interested in psychoanalysis, but as he became disenchanted with its unscientific, untestable claims, he turned to studying brain function. He recently edited an important book, *Psychiatry, Psychoanalysis, and the New Biology of Mind* (Kandel 2005), where he underlines that while we inherit our genes from our species and our family, at any given time many of the genes that potentially affect brain activity may be dormant. 'Epigenetics' is the process by which genes can be turned off or on to produce or 'express' protein products. Among the factors that regulate gene expression are environment and experience; this includes psychotherapy, which changes gene expression and alters neural connections.

ATTACHMENT: THE CONCEPTUAL FRAMEWORK OF NURTURE GROUPS

If we are to work successfully with children experiencing social, emotional and behaviour difficulties, we strongly need to have in our minds a clear theoretical framework for understanding the behaviour and the underlying emotional states. I have spent the last 15 years of my life promoting nurture groups, and it is this experience I shall now draw on to show how we can intervene effectively in children's lives. Nurture groups draw heavily on ideas of attachment, on the way in which the child from birth on relates to its carers and internalises a view of the world. This then shapes the child's reaction to other relationships and also influences the response he or she elicits from those around him or her.

Attachment theory is based on the work of John Bowlby (1988) who, working with children from severely disrupted backgrounds, found that his training in classical psychoanalysis, namely that emotional development is largely the result of libidinal drives within the nuclear family, was quite inadequate to explain or to devise treatment for his patients. He turned to parenting behaviour in other mammals, and stressed the biological need of all young mammals to attach in order to survive.

The interaction between child and carer is intense. From birth on, the child is building up, to quote Bowlby, an 'internalised working model', which we now know will be reflected in their brain development. Children who are neglected, abused, or subject to frequent changes of carer, will feel that the world is a dangerous place, perhaps that they themselves are worthless, that adults are not to be trusted. Once adults understand unacceptable behaviour from that perspective, it is then seen as the child's attempt to have some control over a frightening world. The danger, otherwise, is that what they do can so easily evoke the response they most fear, one that confirms that they are bad, worthless, unlikeable. When the adult carer/teacher learns by empathetic observation to see what lies behind the behaviour, they then seek to give the child a better experience of adults and so begin to change his/her damaging perceptions of self and others. Staff, teachers and assistants, trained in attachment theory, which is central to nurture group work, give warm acceptance, set standards of desirable conduct, and teach in ways accessible to the child at the developmental stage reached. Nurture groups have well-researched success in raising attainments, attendance, self-esteem, improving relationships between children and their parents, and affecting the ethos of the whole school (Cooper and Whitebread 2007).

LOOKING BEHIND THE BEHAVIOUR

A diagnostic scheme that helps people to understand what lies behind the behaviour of children and young people with SEBD has proved immensely popular. It is the Boxall Profile (Bennathan and Boxall 1998), developed by Marjorie Boxall, the founder of nurture groups, in response to teachers' request for a more precise way of assessing need, planning intervention and measuring progress. Its use, together with the understanding of the developmental principles on which nurture group work is based, deepens teachers' understanding of the child's difficulties. As one teacher said: 'Confronted with a child whose anxiety-provoking behaviour makes no sense, the Profile is where you start. It gives you insights and suggests points of entry into the child's world' (Bennathan and Boxall 1998, p.50).

The profile is divided in two sections. The first, Developmental Strands, looks at the child's current stage of learning under various aspects of early development. The second, the Diagnostic Profile, shows behaviours and attitudes that get in the way of the child's learning and relating. This is the part which induces the WOW factor in users. 'Now I understand!'. The Diagnostic Profile is divided into three clusters. The first is Self-limiting Features, which reveal the lack of a normal thrust for growth. The second is Undeveloped Behaviour, where the child's upbringing has not given them the inner resources to enable them to relate well to others and to engage with learning appropriately for their age; this group responds well to help given appropriate to their developmental stage and mostly make rapid progress. The third is Unsupported Development, which indicates whether the child has suffered a profound lack of early nurturing care. These are the children who seem most at risk of developing antisocial behaviour and mental health difficulties in adulthood. Insecurity and fear give way to a thrust for survival. As a protection against hurt and to maintain self-regard, increasingly alienated and negative behaviour appears. Children showing marked features of negativism towards others are motivated by anger, sometimes by rage, as they make their own way; their antisocial behaviour may become an increasingly well-organised, internalised pattern that brings them power and satisfaction and is thus self-perpetuating and motivating (Bennathan and Boxall 1998). It must be obvious that children showing such signs of unhappiness are, unless given skilled help, heading for wasted lives, damaging to themselves and to others.

THE POWER OF ATTACHMENT THEORY

Clearly the concept of attachment is crucial in seeking to understand and support children with social, emotional and behavioural difficulties and help them to grow into healthy adults. It is a very important psychological construct and should form part of the professional armoury of all teachers and carers. There are many schools and units where therapeutic and therefore life-changing care is given. The following example from a nurture group intervention illustrates its therapeutic impact on the life of children in difficulty.

> A drug-dependent mother came to school to collect her five-year-old Stephen. When she saw him she excitedly denied that she knew him and that he was her child; she said she would be accused of taking somebody else's child, and would not take him home. He pleaded in great distress that he really was Stephen. The nurture group teacher protected the child as best she could, calmed the mother down and called the family's social worker who took them home. Two days later the boy returned to school; after the nurture group was settled, he took his teacher firmly by the hand, led her to the mirror, undressed himself completely, inspected his reflection carefully, went to the dressing-up box, dressed himself in costume, inspected himself again, took off the costume, put his clothes back on. All this was deadly serious, no smiles, this was not play, not a word was spoken. He then went back to the work table, and got on with his work. His teacher understood by empathy that she was to say nothing, just be there. This is providing therapy of the highest order. Later he was placed in a loving foster home and began to make steady progress.

The following quotations are excerpts received by the author from two girls and three boys aged 13 to 14 attending a nurture group in a secondary school:

> **Haley:** I came to nurture group because I was miserable and not proud of myself. I was also hiding for a very long time that I couldn't see and it was slowing down my writing and I never got it finished. I have gotten better since then because Sir and Miss always find a way to make me laugh and be happy so I am not miserable and I'm proud of myself. I can now see because I went and got my classes.

> **Katie:** I go to Nurture lessons because I needed to learn about myself and my behaviour, I felt unhappy and I felt ugly. Now I have learnt about myself, behaviour improved a lot – I feel really happy and now I have a modelling job!

> **Barnaby:** Before I came into Nurture, I was always in trouble. Sir and Miss have taught me to control my anger. We have done lots of fun things, food tasting, breakfast club, lunch club and learned lots of new games. If it was not for Mr W— and Mrs S— I would still be in trouble.

John: Before I joined Nurture I had no real friends and nobody knew me for what I am now. I had a past where I was beaten up every day in my primary and secondary schools. When I moved here I was teased, bullied, pushed about and had low self-esteem. I used to walk the corridors alone and acted the class fool to try and get people to like me. Then I joined Nurture. Nurture has been the best highlight of my life. I have learned lots of new and interesting stuff and I no longer care for bullies. You couldn't even imagine what you have done for me. Nurture has rebuilt my life.

Allan: A year ago before I came to Nurture, it wasn't very pleasant being me because I felt unwanted and abandoned. My behaviour was provoking my Mum but I did not realise it until now. Nurture is for me one of the most memorable things I have done and since I have been here I have learnt to find myself. I found out what I could do, things I couldn't do like cook and play an instrument. In my cooking the most exciting thing was well…cooking. In my music it was the sound of me playing it and thinking to myself…

CONCLUSION

There is wide concern throughout our society today about the number of students who leave school with very little in the way of qualifications and at risk of being socially excluded one way or another. So much of this could be prevented if all schools were well informed about the emotional reality of life for many pupils. School is such a formative experience in all our lives that it is our duty as people who know the realities of life for our group of vulnerable children to make clear to the wider society that early neglect of children's emotional needs can prove very costly to society in the long run.

REFERENCES

Bennathan, M. and Boxall, M. (1998) *The Boxall Profile: Handbook for Teachers.* London: Nurture Group Network.

Bowlby, J. (1988) *A Secure Base; Clinical Applications of Attachment Theory.* London: Routledge.

Cooper P. and Whitebread J. (2007) 'The effectiveness of nurture groups on student progress: Evidence from a national research study.' *Emotional and Behavioural Difficulties 12,* 3, 171–190.

Kandel, E.R. (2005) *Psychiatry, Psychoanalysis, and the New Biology of Mind.* Washington, DC: American Psychiatric Publishing.

Rutter, M. *et al.* (2007) 'Effects of profound early institutional deprivation: An overview of findings from a UK longitudinal study of Romanian adoptees.' *European Journal of Developmental Psychology 4,* 3, 332–350.

Watson, J.D. and Crick, F.H.C. (1953) 'Molecular structure for nucleic acids: A structure for deoxyribose nucleic acid.' *Nature 171,* 737–738.

CHAPTER 12

Kangaroo Classes: An Adaptation of Nurture Groups

Caroline Couture

INTRODUCTION

Many primary school students with social, emotional and behaviour difficulties (SEBD) in Quebec, Canada, believe that academic success is a difficult goal to achieve. Over the past 15 years, the number of students with such difficulties has constantly increased even though many educational, administrative and financial measures have been put in place by the education authorities to address the needs of these children (Conseil supérieur de l'éducation 2001). A report from the Ministère de l'Éducation, du Loisir et du Sport (MELS 2006) underlines the importance of organizing educational services based on an individualized approach according to the specific needs of the individual student. Furthermore, the Special Education Policy currently in place (Ministère de l'Éducation 1999) strongly recommends to school boards that they make sure that student services are offered in the most natural context possible.

In spite of these and similar efforts for children with behaviour problems, inclusion in mainstream education classrooms may not be the most effective option. Their type of difficulty often requires a highly structured and predictable environment, which may be hard for schools to provide in a mainstream classroom. In fact, such children often have not developed the level of skills in following the rules and routines of the ordinary classroom shown by their non-SEBD peers, and are easily overwhelmed by the complexity of classroom management systems. This may be partly explained by the fact that emotional

and behavioural difficulties are frequently accompanied by learning difficul-
ties, which may interfere with their ability to absorb and follow rules (Fortin *et al.* 1996). Such children are also often socially isolated (Conseil supérieur de l'éducation 2001) or live in families facing various difficulties. These problems may exacerbate difficulties that they have in integrating with their peers. Furthermore, aggression and violence, exhibited by many of these students, may pose threats to the safety and wellbeing of the other students (Ministère de l'Éducation 1999). This makes it necessary to plan for a combination of spe-
cialized provision where these students can receive education adapted to their needs while aiming at successful integration in the future. The latest available figures in Quebec show that approximately a quarter of the students identified as having social, emotional and behaviour difficulties by the school were taught outside the mainstream class setting (Conseil supérieur de l'éducation 2001; Déry, Toupin *et al.* 2005). According to the Special Education Policy, special classes in mainstream schools are the preferred choice when placement in a mainstream classroom is considered not appropriate, since it allows the student to receive specialized services while still allowing opportunities for students to remain in social contact with their mainstream peers for parts of the day, such as during break and lunch times.

NURTURE GROUPS

Two school boards in Montreal recently adopted an innovative type of special class inspired by a model that has been used in England for the past 30 years to support students with SEBD (Bennathan and Boxall 2000). Nurture groups are an educational provision that is defined as a place of learning specifically organized for students whose problems at school are explained by a need for social and individual experiences resulting from unattended needs during the first years of life (Cooper 2004). The main idea behind this type of provision is greatly influenced by Bowlby's theory of attachment (Bennathan and Boxall 2000). Following the disintegration of the family environment and fragmen-
tation of the care and support received, some children find it very difficult to develop the emotional resources and skills necessary for engagement in recip-
rocal and pro-social relationships with others (i.e. both adults and peers). According to Boxall (2002), it is directly owing to these difficulties that such children experience difficulty in their behaviour at school. As a result, such children benefit from being given experiences in school that help them to develop the skills that many of their mainstream peers already possess (Bennathan and Boxall 2000). In a nurture group, two adults (a teacher and a learning support assistant) try to recreate the educational and caring experi-

ence that the children missed in their first years of life. These adults' behaviour is partly modelled on the relationship that normally exists between a mother and a child, offering care and continuous support, within a protective environment which is carefully controlled (Boxall 2002).

A two-year evaluation study of nurture group conducted by Paul Cooper and colleagues at the University of Leicester indicate that students who attended a nurture group showed more improvement in social, emotional and behaviour skills after four school terms (ie. 1.3 years), than students with similar problems who attended mainstream classrooms in the same schools. The results also indicate that 76 per cent of students attending nurture group are able to apply what they have learnt in the mainstream classroom. Finally, this study shows that nurture groups in operation for at least two years have more impact on the children's behaviour than groups that are in their first or second year of service (Cooper 2004; Cooper and Whitebread 2007).

Kangaroo Classes

Inspired by the nurture group experience, the Marie-Victorin and Vallée-des-Tisserands school boards in Montreal decided to join forces in an action research project to adapt the English model to the Quebec context. This initiative led to the creation of five classes named ' Kangaroo Classes' during the 2005/6 scholastic year. The team chose the term 'kangaroo' to name these classes to refer to the emotional proximity that is developed in them between adults and children. The Quebec Kangaroo Classes (KCs) form part of a mainstream primary school and consist of a group of about ten students with behaviour problems led by a teacher and a learning support assistant. KCs function on the same principles as those that guide the nurture group approach (Bennathan and Boxall 2000).

KCs are, however, different from nurture groups in various ways. First, even though students targeted by nurture groups are children who show signs of early childhood neglect, have experienced severed relationships with key attachment figures (ie. parents or carers), and are unable to learn due to isolation or extreme behaviour problems, students enrolled in KCs were already attending a special class for behaviour problems. Thus, the Quebec model has a more curative and less preventative approach than the British one. Furthermore, students enrolled in KCs come from many different schools within the school board, and for some students the classroom is located geographically far away from their neighbourhood school. These factors made it impossible to preserve a nurture group characteristic that prefers nurture group students to remain in close association with the mainstream classrooms from which they are originally referred. However, a special effort is made in Quebec made to enable KC students to experience inclusion in the mainstream classrooms of the host school, or at least be in frequent contact with students from these classrooms during structured activities. The physical organization, the fact that adults work together with about a dozen children, the presence of routine and a reassuring structure, and the interventions suited to the needs of the students, are however, nurture group characteristics that are preserved in KCs.

It is important to stress that inclusion is a very important principle that differentiates KCs from other types of special classrooms for students with SEBD. The effort put into offering every student the opportunity to experience inclusion allows him or her to maintain an accurate image of the behaviour expected in a mainstream classroom. These experiences also allow him or her to experience success in these classrooms and thereby perceive them as an educational setting that could eventually be within his or her reach. Maintaining contact with mainstream classrooms also allows a gradual transition towards inclusion when the student's developmental progress could possibly allow him or her to learn in that setting. Finally, the presence of a student with difficulties in the mainstream classroom allows both other students and mainstream teachers to understand better the difficulties that these children go through and to learn to regard them as normal human beings.

METHODOLOGY

This chapter describes the findings of a study aimed at evaluating the effectiveness of KCs in relation to the behaviour of children who have attended the classroom in its first year (2005/6). The study is based on standardized measures that evaluated the children's behaviour problems (externalized and internalized) and their emotional and behaviour development. KC students were compared with students receiving their education in mainstream schools. The teachers' and parents' perceptions of the effectiveness of KCs in improving the behaviour of students were taken into consideration. Finally, the amount of time KC students spent in mainstream classrooms was also documented.

The study was carried out with two groups of children between the ages of 6 and 13. The experimental group was made up of all the children enrolled in the five KCs (two from the Marie-Victorin school board and three from the Vallée-des-Tisserands school board) at the beginning of the 2005/6 scholastic year. These children were already enrolled in special classrooms for behaviour problems following the recommendations of an ad hoc committee. Since KCs replaced the existing special classrooms, there was no need to select students for the study. The experimental group comprises 41 children (35 boys and 6 girls) divided amongst the five KC groups.

The control group consisted of students who were identified as having behaviour problems from both the Marie-Victorin and Hautes-Rivières school boards. To avoid any risks of contamination, the students in the control group could not attend schools where KC was implemented. Twenty-six students (25 boys and 1 girl) identified as having behaviour problems were recruited to form the control group, 16 of whom attended special classrooms for behaviour problems and five were included in mainstream classrooms. Both the control and experimental groups were similar with regard to the students' age and socio-economic status (cf. Toupin 1993).

The first wave of testing was carried out in October 2005 when teachers and parents completed various instruments described below. The mainstream class teachers (control group) and the KC teachers and learning support assistants shared the task of assessing the children in their classroom. The two groups of parents received the questionnaires in a sealed envelope. The second wave of testing was carried out in May 2006 in the same manner while making sure that the same adult at school (teacher or learning support assistant) completed the same questionnaires at both assessments. The following aspects were evaluated:

- behaviour (*Child Behavior Checklist* and the *Teacher Report Form* Achenbach and Rescorla 2001)

- social and emotional development. (*Boxall Profile* Bennathan and Boxall 1998)

- perception of impact (parent questionnaire Cooper 2005).

Results

Factor analysis with repeated measures was carried out with time 1 and time 2 assessments of the continuous variables (CBCL and TRF internalized and externalized problems and the sub-scales of Developmental Strands and Diagnostic Profile of the Boxall Profile). These analyses indicated whether the students' problems differed according to the type of services received if the behaviour change between time 1 and time 2 was significant and also if the two groups evolved in a similar or different fashion between both assessments.

Change according to the group

Results concerning internalized and externalized behaviour problems suggest that the two groups changed very little between the two assessments. However, KC students show less internalized problems according to the teacher than students receiving traditional services (control group) at both waves of testing. Furthermore, results of the Developmental Strand section of the Boxall Profile suggest a considerable improvement in most areas in the KC students showing that changes over time were different in both groups. The development of children in KC improves more than the development of children receiving the traditional services, which seems to deteriorate or to remain stable. Specifically, the KC students developed a better attention span, a better ability to establish links between experiences, better interactions and more constructive answers, better understanding of limit setting, and were more secure and cooperative. The ability to adapt to others is the only improvement noticed amongst the control group students, and is also observed amongst the KC students. One must keep in mind, however, that despite these improvements, the behaviour of the students was still below that expected at their age. Finally, results of the Diagnostic Profile section of the Boxall Profile suggest no significant change, except that students from both groups improved their attachment skills during the year.

Parent and teacher perception of the effectiveness of Kangaroo Classes

When asked about the effectiveness of KC, more than 80 per cent of the parents thought that they had a positive or very positive effect on their child's education, behaviour at school, and feelings towards self and school. Furthermore, 78.6 per cent believed that they also had a positive effect on their child's behaviour at home while 71.4 per cent believed that KC helped to improve their relationship with their child. Finally, very few parents believed that KC could have had a negative effect on their child.

Similarly the teachers believed that the KC had a positive or very positive influence on more than 85 per cent of the students on the following variables: behaviour at school, feelings about oneself, attitude towards school, the relationship between the teacher and the student and collaboration between parents and school. Furthermore, 77.8 per cent of the teachers said that KC had a positive effect on the students' education. The teachers believed that KC had a negative effect only in the education of one student and in the behaviour of another.

Time spent in mainstream classrooms

Of the 35 KC students involved at time 2, 77.1 per cent spent some time in a mainstream classroom. On average, the students spent 6.85 hours per week included with their peers in the mainstream, which is more than one school day. Of the 27 students, 29.4 per cent spent less than 3 hours in mainstream education, 53 per cent spent between 3 and 5 hours, while 17.7 per cent spent between 22 and 25 hours.

Discussion

The results obtained from the standardized questionnaires suggest that generally very little improvement occurred in the behaviour of the students taking part in the study, either in KC or in mainstream schools. It was evident that the behaviour of both the children in KCs and those attending other types of provision did not change over time. At first glance, these results may not seem very encouraging, but we must nonetheless note that the behaviour of students attending KCs, at least, did not deteriorate. Based on the results of the control group, other types of services offered to students with similar behaviour profiles did not have better results either.

It is important to keep in mind, however, that the small number of children in each group might not have favoured the detection of significant differences between groups and over time. Moreover, it frequently occurs that the impact of an intervention may not be observed on standardized tests, especially when these are filled by people close to the child. The results of Cooper and Whitebread (2007) indicated that nurture groups implemented for two years and over were more effective in improving the behaviour of the students. This implies that evaluation of KCs would have to take place over a longer period of time than that in the present study in order to assess their effectiveness on student behaviour. It would probably be necessary for many students in our sample to participate in KCs for over a year to observe an improvement in their behaviour, especially if we consider that many of them have had a long history of problems at school.

Furthermore, the results of the Boxall Profile that tend to support the effectiveness of KC, seem to support this type of interpretation since many effects were found in the Developmental Strand of the Boxall Profile, a section measuring expected behaviour of students in school. Therefore, it seems that students in KC have made more progress on many developmental tasks that allowed them to function better at school than students enrolled in other types of provision. These results support the intervention hypothesis that when children enact typical experiences of the first years of life in a secure and predictable environment, they are able to continue their developmental stages that they were unable to accomplish successfully during their early years. KCs seem to be a setting that is more favourable for this type of development than other services for children with behaviour problems.

The fact that none of the sub-scales of the Diagnostic Profile, describing behaviour that blocks or interferes with a student's satisfactory engagement in school, show improvement over time, suggest that children must first develop their ability to interact with others and understand the world that surrounds them before any noticeable change in behaviour can take place. Within such a perspective, problem behaviour may thus be seen as a way to defend oneself against the world in which one lives (Bennathan and Boxall 1998). It is therefore indicative that for the children who attend KC for over a year, the results on the Diagnostic Profile sub-scales could eventually decrease significantly.

Even though the results of the standardized tests do not show any impact on the KC students, the perceptions of parents and teachers are much more positive; both parents and teachers believe that KC had a positive effect on the students. These results suggest that, despite the lack of apparent positive change according to the standardized tests, adults who regularly interact with children in KCs observed notable changes at academic, behaviour, emotional and interpersonal levels. We do not exclude a similar conclusion for the students in the control group, and it is possible that the results were positive for them as well. We can nonetheless conclude that KCs are perceived as a useful and effective provision for students with SEBD according to both parents and teachers.

A distinctive characteristic of KC is the importance given to the inclusion of the students in mainstream classrooms. The great majority of students were given this opportunity, with more than 70 per cent of the children spending more than three hours per week in mainstream classrooms. Inclusion is clearly a distinctive characteristic of KCs, which place this type of provision in accordance with the Special Education Policy (Ministère de l'Éducation 1999) that recommends education in the most natural environment possible. If full inclusion could not yet be achieved for most KC students because of the severity of their behaviour problems, at least the KC allowed these students as much as possible the opportunity to have the same academic and social experiences as mainstream students. It is important to mention that the integration periods were carefully organized to allow the students to succeed by including them in activities where they could make the most out of their strengths. Furthermore, on those rare occasions where a student manifested behaviour difficulties in the mainstream classroom, he or she was rapidly accompanied back to the safety base at the KC and the episode was discussed in order to help him or her succeed next time.

CONCLUSION

The results presented in this chapter must be considered in the light of certain methodological limitations. First, it was not possible randomly to divide the participants between the two groups, and recruiting was done through convenience rather than random sampling. However, this limitation is considered justified when evaluating any service already in existence in an educational organization. It must also be borne in mind that this was the first year of the KCs and thus the professionals who worked in the KCs became more knowledgeable and skilled with time and consequently their practice was set to improve. It is one of the reasons that we hypothesized that the effects of KC on the students' behaviour would be greater in the following years.

We believe that the results shown here place KCs amongst the promising educational provision for students with SEBD. As the Special Education Policy mentions for students with difficulties, it may sometimes be necessary to accept that success can be interpreted in different ways depending on the needs and the abilities of the students. For some, it may mean taking a certain amount of time to help them acquire the skills and behaviours necessary to prepare them to face the academic world. The strict pathway that keeps them restricted to a system that is not suited to their needs and where they lack the necessary skills to cope academically and socially, can simply mean placing them in a situation of continual failure, emphasizing their difficulties instead of their strengths and abilities that are just waiting to be developed given the appropriate educational context.

REFERENCES

Achenbach, T.M. and Rescorla, L.A. (2001) *Manual for the ASEBA School-Age Forms and Profiles*. Burlington, VT: University of Vermont, Research Center for Children, Youth, and Families.

Bennathan, M. and Boxall, M. (1998) *The Boxall Profile: Handbook for Teachers*. London: Nurture Group Network.

Bennathan, M. and Boxall, M. (2000) *Effective Intervention in Primary Schools: Nurture Groups* (2nd edition). London: David Fulton.

Boxall, M. (2002) *Nurture Groups in School: Principles and Practice*. London: Paul Chapman.

Conseil supérieur de l'éducation (2001) *Les élèves en difficulté de comportement à l'école primaire: Comprendre, prévenir, intervenir*. Québec: Conseil supérieur de l'éducation.

Cooper, P. (2005) *Nurtire Groups: Parent Questionnaire*. Leicester: University of Leicester.

Cooper, P. (2004) 'Nurture Groups: The research evidence.' In J. Wearmouth, R.C. Richmond and T. Glynn (eds) *Addressing Pupils' Behaviour: Responses at District, School and Individual Levels*. London: David Fulton.

Cooper, P. and Whitebread, D. (2007) 'The effectiveness of nurture groups on student progress: Evidence from a national research study.' *Emotional and Behavioural Difficulties 12*, 3, 171–190.

Déry, M., Toupin, J., Pauzé, R. and Verlaan, P. (2005) 'Les caractéristiques d'élèves en difficultés de comportement placés en classe spéciale ou intégrés dans la classe ordinaire.' *Revue Canadienne de l'Éducation 28*, 23–46.

Fortin, L., Toupin, J., Pauzé, R., Déry, M. and Mercier, H. (1996) 'Variables associées à la compétence scolaire des adolescents en troubles de comportement.' *Scientia Paedagogica Experimentalis 33*, 2, 245–267.

Ministère de l'Éducation , du Loisir et du Sport (2006) *L'organisation des services éducatifs aux élèves à risque et aux élèves handicapés ou en difficulté d'adaptation ou d'apprentissage (EHDAA)*. Quebec: Gouvernement du Québec.

Ministère de l'Éducation (1999) *Une école adaptée à tous ses élèves. Prendre le virage du succès. Politique de l'adaptation scolaire*. Quebec: Gouvernement du Québec.

Toupin, J. (1993) *Indice de statuts socio-économique*. Sherbrooke: Groupe de recherche sur les inadaptations sociales de l'enfance (GRISE), Université de Sherbrooke.

CHAPTER 13

Aggression Replacement Training: Decreasing Behaviour Problems by Increasing Social Competence

Knut Gundersen and Frode Svartdal

INTRODUCTION

Research evidence suggests a causal connection between lack of social and emotional competence and difficulties such as loneliness (Jones, Hobbs, and Hockenbury 1982), depression (Tse and Bond 2004), bullying and aggression (DeRosier 2004) as well as drug and alcohol abuse (Gaffney *et al.* 1998). A causal relationship has also been identified between children's ability to develop friendships and the degree of life-long mental health problems (Hay, Payne, and Chadwick 2004). Lack of social skills has also been found to contribute to behaviour problems in persons with autism (Njardvik, Matson and Cherry 1999) and mental disability (Patel 2004). The strong correlation between positive changes in socio-emotional competence and decrease in behaviour difficulties (Najaka, Gottfredson and Wilson 2001) also indicates that training in emotional competence should be one of the key strategies for dealing with social, emotional and behaviour difficulties. In this respect, the growing emphasis on training programmes in this area in both schools and institutions has positive implications.

Gottfredson (1997) concluded that the most effective programmes that address behaviour problems are those that include 'a range of social competency skills e.g. developing self control, stress management, responsible decision making, social problem solving, and communication skills' (p.55). Further, Sørlie (2000) found that the most promising intervention for behaviour problems is the training in a broad spectrum of social skills in relation to peers and adults, combined with the correction of the behaviour problems (see Gundersen and Svartdal 2006).

AGGRESSION REPLACEMENT TRAINING

Aggression replacement training (ART) (Goldstein, Glick and Gibbs 1998) is one of the interventions that are gaining momentum in Norway as well as in other European and trans-Atlantic countries. ART is a programme developed over a 15-year period by Arnold Goldstein and his colleagues at the Center for Aggression Research, Syracuse University, USA. The programme has gradually been developed and adapted to different age groups and specific problem areas, including parents who have abused children (Goldstein *et al.* 1985) and drug addicts (Goldstein *et al.* 1990). It has its roots in operant theory, behaviour modification and behaviour therapy, social learning theory, cognitive therapy and cognitive behavioral analysis. Most social competence training programmes are rooted within such a framework and are often denoted as cognitive behavioural and cognitive approaches (Andreassen 2005; Hollin 2004).

ART is one of the best-validated programmes in its field (Barnoski and Aos 2004; Gundersen and Svartdal 2006; Nugent and Bruley 1998; Nugent, Bruley and Winimaki 1999) and has been used both as a primary prevention measure and as an intervention for persons with severe behavioral disorders. The conclusion from a research-based evaluation of current programmes for behaviour problems in Norway (Nordahl *et al.* 2006) has been that 'the program has been evaluated as belonging to category 3: Programs with documented effects. The research group recommends ART in lower secondary schools for those groups which have developed, or are in danger of developing, behavior problems' (p.17). ART is also recommended for children and adolescents with behaviour problems living in residential homes (Andreassen 2005) and currently the Norwegian Ministry for Children and Equality has built six new research institutions which include ART as one of their main components.

Rationale and components of programme

The rationale behind the development of ART is to help participants in establishing new prosocial behaviours to replace previous problematic behaviour patterns, particularly verbal or physical aggression and withdrawal. Anger is a natural emotion that may be regarded as a defence mechanism to protect oneself when feeling threatened. It is not until it reaches a level where it prevents one from making rational assessments of the actual situation, resulting in inappropriate aggression, that it becomes dysfunctional. ART seeks to help the individual control the negative impact of anger and use its energy in positive ways. It focuses on the emotional, cognitive and behavioural processes involved in controlling anger and replacing with more adaptive behaviour.

Aggression replacement training is a multimodal programme and consists of three components, namely anger control, prosocial skills training and moral reasoning. Anger control training (the affective or emotional component) entails young people being trained to recognize their external and internal triggers for aggression and to control anger using various techniques. Social skills training (the action component) focuses on training various structured skills, ranging from simple (e.g. listening to someone else, starting a conversation) to more complex ones (e.g. avoiding disruption, handling group pressure). Generally, research shows that individuals with behaviour difficulties score poorly on social skills tests, and that training in such skills leads to enhanced social perception, social cognition and social performance which in turn lead to an improvement in prosocial behaviour (Robinson and Porporino 2001).

In moral reasoning training (the thought and values component), participants are given training in dealing with challenging ethical and moral dilemmas, and in handling situations in their own lives in line with their moral and ethical values. Through cognitive restructuring strategies, the participants are helped to identify irrational thought patterns, such as cognitive distortions or self-centred thinking like blaming others, minimizing/mislabeling and assuming the worst in a situation, and replace them with a more rational understanding and assessment of the situation. The individual is encouraged to develop alternative thought patterns or self-instructions that help both reduce the conflict and *create* 'mental distance' from the anger triggers (Feindler and Baker 2004).

Even if the three components are trained separately, elements of each are partly integrated in the others (e.g. social skills as part of anger control training). Training takes place in groups of five to eight participants. Groups are matched in terms of age, similarity of behaviour challenges and friendship between participants. Elliot and Gresham (1991) also recommend the inclusion of group members with a higher level of social competence as positive role models. Two trainers conduct ART sessions. Rules and consequences for behaviour infractions are clearly defined. Participation is voluntary, and the use of positive reinforcement and small non-competitive games, are highly recommended to secure the motivation of participants. There is a firm structure in the programme, including defining the theme of the session, demonstration, role-playing, questioning where and when to use the skill, feedback/evaluation and homework. Goldstein *et al.* (1998) recommend that the three components of the programme are scheduled for training at least once a week over a period of ten weeks. In order to transfer and maintain skills, it is important to establish contact with important individuals (family members, teachers, club leaders) in the participants' social environments (Gundersen and Svartdal 2006).

EFFECTIVENESS OF ART TRAINING IN NORWAY

In Norway, ART has been making continuous inroads in the past five years and has been used in preschool centres (Dolmen 2005), primary schools (Dolmen and Solid 2005), junior secondary schools (Onsager 2005), and child welfare institutions (Hellerdal 2005; Olsen and Boutera 2005). A slightly modified ART programme has also been used with young persons with Asperger's syndrome (Husby and Sagstad 2005) and autism (Moynahan 2003).

The ART Centre at Diakonhjemmet University College in Oslo has developed a postgraduate programme in Training in Social Competencies with ART as the main subject. The ART Centre offers also a short training course in ART for teachers, seminars in Family ART for children and their family, and courses in Junior ART-trainers, which involves training young people with former behaviour problems to become trainers for peers (Olsen and Boutera 2005; Finne, Olsen and Gundersen 2008).

As a part of its postgraduate training course in Social Competence at Diakonhjemmet University College, the students undertake a 30-session ART training programme for children and adolescents with behaviour problems. Two studies have been carried out to evaluate the effectiveness of the programme. In the first study, (Gundersen and Svartdal 2006), 11 groups of students performed a 24-session ART intervention programme as part of their studies. The participants included 65 children and young persons with varying degrees of behaviour problems. Forty-seven participants received the ART programme, whereas 18 received standard social and educational services and served as control subjects. Social problems and skills were assessed before and after the ART intervention using multi-informant instruments, namely the Social Skills Rating System (Gresham and Elliot 1990), the Child and Adolescent Disruptive Behaviour Inventory (Burns, Taylor and Rusby 2001), the How I Think Questionnaire (Barriga *et al.* 2001) and the Achenbach System of Empirically Based Assessment (Achenbach and Rescorla 2001).

Post-intervention, the ART group showed significant improvement on nine of the eleven outcome measures following the intervention, both in terms of increased social skills and reduced behaviour problems. Generally the parents reported more improvement in behaviour problems than the teachers, while improvements in social skills were equally perceived by both teachers and parents. There were also significant positive changes in the self-report scales for problem behaviour, but not on the measure of social skills. On the other hand, with two exceptions, there was little improvement in behaviour amongst the participants in the control group. The results from the self-report scales were less clear. One of the reasons was that the young people had problems in filling out the questionnaires.

Results from the second study (Gundersen and Svartdal 2008) indicate similar conclusions. This study was carried out by the same authors and involved 140 children and young persons. The preliminary findings were quite similar to those of the first study, with significant changes in the predicted direction in 13 of 19 measures, while the control group participants obtained significant changes in the same direction as in the ART groups in only two of the 19 measures.

The conclusions from these two studies confirm that ART has been found to be effective in reducing behaviour problems and increasing socio-emotional skills in children and young persons with behaviour difficulties. However, the positive changes in the control group went contrary to prediction, and three hypotheses have been suggested to explain this finding, namely test-retest effect (repeated administration of same tests); diffusion of intervention (ART interventions directed at the ART groups also affected control subjects); and model effects (behaviour changes in models in the ART groups affected subjects in the control groups). After eliminating the test-retest hypothesis by testing for changes without intervention, diffusion of treatment and model effects are probably the most likely explanations. If true, effects (especially the model effect) in the control groups should be most pronounced in projects with pronounced effects in the ART group. The correlation between change indices in the ART and control groups was quite high ($r = .58$), indicating that participants in the control group were affected in a positive direction to a larger extent if the change in the ART group was significant.

Our findings also indicate that programmes like ART could be carried out with young people with various levels of socio-emotional competence. This heterogeneity of competence makes it easier to establish a positive climate in the group and is likely to lead to more positive behaviour amongst young people with behaviour problems though role-modeling. More research, however, needs to be undertaken to establish the impact of such role-modeling on behaviour change. This also includes the effect of using 'junior ART-trainers'; that is, young persons with previous behaviour problems, as role-models for younger peers during ART sessions.

CONCLUSION

ART is spreading very quickly both in Norway and other European countries. Even if there is a need of more studies to measure its effect in larger-scale studies, the two studies described above and the more anecdotal evidence, suggest that ART works. The research group appointed by the Norwegian Ministry for Children and Equality (Nordahl *et al.* 2006) and the research programme in the Norwegian services for residential homes for children, both agreed that ART is useful and effective in supporting the behaviour change of children and young people with behaviour difficulties. The programme has now been translated into Polish, Dutch, Norwegian, Swedish, English, Icelandic and Russian. There are also plans to include other components in the programme, such as situational perception training and problem-solving. Even if it is promising, more effort should be made to ensure more rigorous and faithful implementation of the programme. This includes adequate training, with at least eight days training for teachers, and supervision and monitoring of trainers. More effort should also be made to facilitate the generalization of the programme skills to applied contexts in real life.

REFERENCES

Achenbach, T.M. and Rescorla, L.A. (2001) *Manual for the ASEBA School-Age Forms and Profiles.* Burlington, VT: University of Vermont, Research Center for Children, Youth, and Families.

Andreassen, T. (2005) 'Aggression Replacement Training (ART) som del av behandlingstilbud i institusjoner for ungdom med alvorlige atferdsvansker.' In B. Stroemgren, L. Moynahan and K. Gundersen (eds) *Erstatt aggresjonen: Aggression Replacement Training og positive atferds- og stottetiltak.* Oslo: Undiversitetsforlaget.

Barnoski, R. and Aos, S. (2004) *Outcome Evaluations of Washington States' Research-Based Programs for Juvenile Offenders* (Rep. No. 04-01-1201). Washington State Institute for Public Policy.

Barriga, A.Q., Gibbs, J.C., Potter, G.B. and Liau, A.K. (2001) *How I Think (HIT) Questionnaire Manual.* Champaign, IL: Research Press.

Burns, G.L., Taylor, T.K. and Rusby, J.C. (2001) *Child and Adolescent Disruptive Behavior Inventory 2.3: Parent Version.* Pullman: Washington State University, Department of Psychology.

DeRosier, M.E. (2004) 'Building relationships and combating bullying: Effectiveness of a school-based social skills group intervention.' *Journal of Clinical Child and Adolescent Psychology 33,* 196–201.

Dolmen, E. and Sollid, G. (2005) 'ARTig i Larvik kommune.' In B.m.l.Strømgren and K. Gundersen (eds) *Erstatt aggresjonen. Aggression Replacement Training og positive atferds-og støttetiltak.* Oslo: Universitetsforlaget.

Domen, E. (2005) 'MiniART i Vårtun Barnehage.' In B.m.l.Strømgren and K. Gundersen (eds) *Erstatt aggresjonen. Aggression Replacement Training og positive atferds- og støttetiltak.* Oslo: Universitetsforlaget.

Elliot, S.N. and Gresham, F.M. (1991) Social skills intervention guide: Practical strategies for social skills training. Circle Pines, MN: American Guidance.

Feinder, E.L. and Baker, K. (2004) 'Anger Management Interventions with Youth'. In Goldstein, A., Nensèn, R., Daleflody, B. and Kait, M. (eds) *New Perspectives on Agression Replacement Training*. Chichester: John Wiley and Sons.

Finne, J., Olsen, T.M. and Gundersen, K. (2008) *Manual for Junior ART Trainers.* Unpublished.

Gaffney, L.R., Thorpe, K., Young, R., Collett, R. and Occhipinti, S. (1998) 'Social skills, expectancies, and drinking in adolescents.' *Addictive Behaviours 23*, 587–599.

Goldstein, A. P. (1990) *Delinquents on Delinquency.* Champaign, IL: Research Press.

Goldstein, A. P., Erné, D., and Keller, H. (1985) *Changing the Abusive Parent.* Champaign, IL: Research Press.

Goldstein, A.P., Glick, B. and Gibbs, J.C. (1998) *Aggression Replacement Training: A Comprehensive Intervention for Aggressive Youth* (Rev. edition). Champaign, IL: Research Press.

Gottfredson, D. (1997) 'School-based Crime Prevention.' In L.W. Sherman *et al.* (eds) *Preventing Crime: What Works, What Doesn't, What's Promising: A Report to the United States Congress.* Washington, DC: Department of Justice, Office of Justice Programs.

Gresham, F.M. and Elliot, S.N. (1990) *Social Skills Rating System.* Circle Pines, MN: American Guidance Service.

Gundersen, K. and Svartdal, F. (2006) 'Aggression replacement training in Norway: Outcome evaluation of 11 Norwegian student projects.' *Scandinavian Journal of Educational Research 50*, 63–81.

Gundersen, K and Svartdal, F. (2008) *Diffusion of treatment interventions: Exploration of 'secondary' treatment diffusion.* Submitted for publication.

Hay, D.F., Payne, A. and Chadwick, A. (2004) 'Peer relations in childhood.' *Journal of Child Psychology and Psychiatry 45*, 84–108.

Hellerdal, S. (2005) 'Implementering av ART i en barnevernsinstitusjon. In B.m.l.Strømgren and K. Gundersen (eds) *Erstatt aggresjonen. Aggression Replacement Training og positive atferds-og støttetiltak.* Oslo: Universitetsforlaget.

Hollin, C. R. (2004) 'The Cognitive-Behavioral Context.' In C.L.Hollin and M. McMurran (eds) *New Perspectives on Aggression Replacement Training.* Chichester: John Wiley & Sons.

Husby, H. and Sagstad, U. (2005) 'ART i avdeling for individuell tilrettelagt opplæring i videregående skole.' In B.m.l.Strømgren and K. Gundersen (eds) *Erstatt aggresjonen. Aggression Replacement Training og positive atferds- og støttetiltak.* Oslo: Universitetsforlaget.

Jones, W.H., Hobbs, S.A. and Hockenbury, D. (1982) 'Loneliness and social skill deficits.' *Journal of Personality and Social Psychology 42*, 682–689.

Moynahan, L. (2003) 'Enhanced aggression replacement training with children and youth with autism spectrum disorder.' *Reclaiming Children and Youth 12*, 3, 174–180.

Najaka, S.S., Gottfredson, D.C. and Wilson, D.B. (2001) 'A meta-analytic inquiry into the relationship between selected risk factors and problem behavior.' *Prevention Science, 2*, 257–271.

Njardvik, U., Matson, J.L. and Cherry, K.E. (1999) 'A comparison of social skills in adults with autistic disorder, pervasive developmental disorder not otherwise specified, and mental retardation.' *Journal of Autism and Developmental Disorders 29*, 287–295.

Nordahl, T., Gravrok, Ø., Knutsmoen, H., Larsen, T. and Rørnes, K. (2006) *Evaluations of Programmes for the Prevention of Behavior Problems and for the Development of Social Competence.* Oslo: Department of Education.

Nugent, W. R. and Bruley, C. (1998) 'The effects of aggression replacement training on antisocial behavior in a runaway shelter.' *Research on Social Work Practice 8*, 6, 637–657.

Nugent, W. R., Bruley, C. and Winimaki, L. (1999) 'The effects of aggression replacement traning on male and female antisocial behavior.' *Research on Social Work Practice 9*, 4, 466–482.

Olsen, T.M. and Boutera, M. (2005) 'Kongsberg-ART (K-ART). Med en arbeidsplass som behandlingsarena.' In B. Strømgren, L. Moynahan and K. Gundersen (eds) *Erstatt aggresjonen: Aggression Replacement Training og positive atferds- og støttetiltak.* Oslo: Universitetsforlaget.

Onsager, T. (2005) 'ART på Hafslund Ungdomsskole i Sarpsborg.' In B.m.l.Strømgren and K. Gundersen (eds) *Erstatt aggresjonen. Aggression Replacement Training og positive atferds-og støttetiltak.* Oslo: Universitetsforlaget.

Patel, N.M. (2004) 'The impact of social-cognitive skills on social competence in persons with mental retardation.' *Dissertation Abstract International: Section B: The Sciences & Engineering. 65.* 1560. US: Univ Microfilms International

Sørlie, M-A. (2000) *Alvorlige atfersproblemer og lovende tiltak i skolen. En forskningsbasert kunnskapsanalyse.* Oslo: Praksis Forlag.

Tse, W.S. and Bond, A.J. (2004) 'The impact of depression on social skills.' *Journal of Nervous and Mental Disorders 192,* 260–268.

Conclusion

From the Needs of Children to the Need for Children: Contemporary Values and Their Implications for the Social and Emotional Wellbeing of Children

Paul Cooper and Carmel Cefai

INTRODUCTION

The preceding chapters have dealt with the needs that children and young people have in relation to the development of social and emotional competence. Core themes of the book have been:

- the importance of empirically based approaches for dealing with social, emotional and behaviour difficulties

- the importance of diversity of provision

- the fundamental significance of the voices of disengaged youngsters

- the importance of emotion-based approaches to education.

Appropriately, the contributors to this book have focused on these issues in relation to primarily educational settings. In this final chapter we broaden the discussion by giving consideration to the wider cultural context that surrounds education. In this way we emphasise the point that educational provision does not exist within a vacuum. Professionals who work with children exist within the same cultural landscape occupied by the children they work with and their parents. Whilst this landscape is diverse, it contains certain dominant features that influence government policy and professional practice in subtle ways, as well as influencing the values and orientations of individuals. We will argue that there is a need for greater awareness of these influences as well as a strong commitment among policy makers and professionals to help limit the negative effects certain cultural trends have on the social and emotional development of children and young people.

THE 'CHILDREN PROBLEM'
Historical developments

As Cunningham (2006) points out, in his social history of childhood since the middle-ages: '[there] is a constant refrain in the history of childhood: children behaved better in previous generations and remained children for much longer' (p.36). He offers numerous examples from contemporaneous documents to illustrate the preoccupation with childhood indiscipline throughout the ages, and highlights the relationship between this concern and the use of coercive approaches to child rearing and behaviour management. The adage: 'spare the rod and spoil the child' appears to have been a consistent and dominant philosophy in the history of child rearing.

Cunningham is also keen to remind us, however, that there have long been powerful voices arguing against this coercive approach. He illustrates this point with reference to a dialogue between St Anselm (the mediaeval Archbishop of Canterbury) and an abbot, who was expressing concern that the boys in his charge remained unruly 'brutes', in spite of the constant beatings that he and his colleagues administered to them. St Anselm's response will have contemporary resonance for readers of this book for its use of the metaphor of horticultural nurturing (see Chapters 10, 11 and 12):

> [St Anselm:] Now tell me, my lord abbot, if you plant a tree shoot in your garden, and straightway shut it in on every side so that it has no space to put out its branches, what kind of tree will you have in after years when you let it out of its confinement?

> [the abbot:] A useless one, certainly, with its branches all twisted and knotted.

> [St Anselm:] And whose fault would this be, except for your own for shutting it in so unnaturally? Without doubt this is what you do with your boys. ...you so terrify them and hem them in on all sides with

treats and blows that they are utterly deprived of their liberty. And being thus so injudicially oppressed, they harbour and welcome and nurse within themselves evil and crooked thoughts like thorns, and cherish those thoughts so passionately that they doggedly reject everything which could minister to their correction. Hence, feeling no love or pity, goodwill or tenderness in your attitude towards them, they have future no faith in your goodness but believe that all your actions proceed from hatred and malice against them.

(Quoted in Cunningham 2006, p.29)

This view of the child's moral character being shaped by the social environment and the importance of caring and nurturing in producing honest and well-adjusted people is reflected in the philosophical deliberations of Rousseau (Aries 1973) and the pioneering work of reformers who worked with deprived and delinquent children in the 19th century, such as Mary Carpenter and Dr Barnardo (Bridgeland 1971). The 20th century saw a continuance of this tradition in the seminal work of Sigmund Freud and his followers in the psychodynamic school, and in the work of inspirational people in the fields of education and child care, such as A.S. Neile (see Neill 1968) and David Wills. The title of one of Wills' many inspirational books, based on his extensive professional experience of setting up and running communities for deprived, disturbing and often delinquent children and young people, sums up succinctly a key tenet of education and child care that can be traced directly back to St Anselm (via Sigmund Freud): *Throw Away Thy Rod* (Wills 1963).

By the 1970s there was growing body of social and psychological research evidence which was found to be in accord with what might be termed this 'therapeutic' or 'nurturing' tradition. The UK's massive longitudinal National Child Development Study, which was begun in the late 1950s, was the basis for Pringle's (1975) theory of the four basic needs of children, which emphasised the relationship between healthy social and psychological development and the need for the following conditions to be met during early childhood:

- love and security
- encouragement and rewards for positive achievement
- new experiences
- to be trusted and to be given responsibilities.

Numerous other needs theories have been developed before and since Pringle's work in this area (see Olsen and Cooper 2001), the unifying feature of which is summed in St Anselm's plea for 'good will and tenderness' as a cornerstone to effective intervention with children, whether it be in the context of parenting, education or rehabilitation. It is also important to note that contemporary theory suggests that 'good will and tenderness' are most effective in contributing to psychological health and prosocial behaviour when they are combined with clear behavioural boundaries (Olsen and Cooper 2001). Or, as St Anselm might have put it, when young people believe that the adults who seek to influence their behaviour hold predominantly positive feelings towards them, they are more likely to accept their guidance and to allow their thinking and behaviour to be influenced.

There has never been, of course, (and probably never will be) a simple relationship between well-wrought ideas, borne out of rational and sensitive reflection, and what passes for 'common sense'. Policy and practice in the area of child care and education remains greatly influenced by commonsense thinking rooted in experience that is interpreted through, at best, folk wisdom (e.g. 'spare the rod, spoil the child'). This may account for the fact that 900 years elapsed before St Anselm's enlightened view of child management was reflected in the abolition of corporal punishment in UK schools in 1982 (Cunningham 2006). Though, to this day, the physical chastisement of children in the UK and other countries in Europe amongst others, remains permissible under law.

The contemporary picture

Perhaps the most pernicious contemporary legacy of the coercive 'spare the rod' philosophy is the active use of what is variously referred to as 'suspension', 'expulsion' or 'exclusion' as a legally sanctioned punitive response to challenging behaviour in schools. This practice is common throughout the world. Whilst it can be argued that social exclusion can be employed as an appropriate and effective intervention, as in the use of 'time out' (Embry and Biglan 2008), any behavioural intervention that relies upon the withdrawal of positive attention depends for its effectiveness on the prior availability of caring and positive attention, the suspension of which gives 'time out' its therapeutic power. Unfortunately, there is reason to believe that the social exclusion of school students who are disruptive is not driven by therapeutic concerns, but is more often an expression of primitive adult reactions rooted in complex and ambivalent, often tacit and unacknowledged, feelings about the nature and value of childhood.

Some readers may find this assertion difficult to accept, and it must be acknowledged that there is no empirical evidence to support this point, in the strictest sense. Indirect support for this argument, however, can be drawn from the fact that published empirical sources focusing on disruptive, acting-out behaviour among school students, far outweigh sources dealing with 'acting in' problems. This is demonstrated in a recent review of research by Schoenfeld and Janney (2008), who identified only eight empirical articles published over the previous 20 years that dealt with the academic effects of anxiety disorders. The serious academic effects associated with anxiety disorders cited in this paper include:

- academic impairment and relatively low levels of achievement among anxious children compared with children in the general population

- teacher perceptions of academic difficulties among anxious students on a par with those of children with externalising difficulties

- difficulties reported by anxious students in performing school-based tasks, including giving oral reports, concentration and completing homework tasks

- anxious students being more likely to opt out of schooling owing to feelings of anxiety.

This points to the conclusion that students with internalising problems are of less concern than those who are disruptive, even though, from an educational perspective, these two groups are in equal need of intervention.

An inescapable inference is that the concerns that adults often express about the behaviour of children and young people reflect a reaction against the negative impact of children's behaviour on adults, rather than a concern for the child. The 'spare the rod, spoil the child' rhetoric suggests that children should be beaten, primarily, for their own good. If this were the genuine motivation for such punitive approaches, however, then we would expect to see an equal level of concern over the problems experienced by the withdrawn, acting-in children, and a well-developed and widespread set of strategies designed to deal with these issues. This is evidently not the case. It seems, therefore, that the coercion and control of children remain key objectives shared by some adults. Sadly, coercive approaches to the management of children tend to lead to the development of coercive social styles in children, an observation made already by St Anselm as well as by contemporary researchers (e.g. Patterson, Reid and Dishion 1992).

It would be completely inaccurate, however, if we were to conclude that attitudes to children have not changed considerably in the last 900 years. This book is in itself a testimony to modern (current?) preoccupations with the welfare and care of children. The concept of 'child protection' is enshrined in the constitutions of civilised societies and communities, and in the UN Convention on the Rights of the Child (1989). The view that the legal construct of 'human rights' should embrace specific 'children's rights' is acknowledged by governments throughout the world (Layard and Dunn 2009). In this respect, the philosophical inheritance of St Anselm, Freud and the pioneers of enlightened approaches to care and education of children and young people, have clearly made their mark.

However, as Layard and Dunn (2009) argue, on the basis of international research literature:

> ...there...is widespread unease about our children's experience – about the commercial pressures they face, the violence they are exposed to, the stresses at school, and the increased emotional distress. Some of this unease is exaggerated and reflects unwarranted angst about the greater freedom children now enjoy. But some of it reflects a greater fear on behalf of our children – that somehow their lives are becoming more difficult, and more difficult than they ought to be. (pp.1–2)

These authors cite UNICEF research evidence that 21st-century children in two of the richest countries in the world (the UK and USA) exhibit rising levels of emotional stress and behavioural disturbance that appear to coincide with increasing problems in the family, peer group and school settings. Furthermore, it is shown that children's physical health is declining, particularly in relation to obesity, and the poverty-gap is widening, with the numbers of children living in economically deprived households being higher in the USA and UK than in other Western countries. Other sources support Layard and Dunn's contention that increasing national prosperity seems, in some cultures at least, to equate with a decline in social and emotional wellbeing of children and young people (Gibson-Cline 1996; James 2007, 2008; Rutter and Smith 1995).

Today children are not subject to the same degree of physical coercion as might once have been the case. They exist, however, in a world that exposes them to pressures and stressors they are ill-equipped to deal with.

WHY ARE CHILDREN IN THIS SITUATION?

In the foregoing section we underlined two main issues. First, children and young people have always been and continue to be subject to coercive efforts by adults to control their behaviour. Second, more enlightened views of the needs of children that stress children's need for caring relationships and nurturing experiences seem to coincide with an increase in the very problems that they seek to address. Explanations for this state of affairs tend to highlight cultural factors. The shift away from collectivist values, which emphasise social responsibility and the role of the individual within the group, and the move towards individualism, which locates self-actualisation as the pinnacle of human achievement, have led to serious problems for children and young people. Layard and Dunn (2009) cite the 'the individual pursuit of private interest and success' as major causes of problems that contribute to the social, emotional and behavioural difficulties manifested by children, such as: 'high [levels of] family break up, teenage unkindness, unprincipled advertising, too much competition in education and…our acceptance of income inequality.' (p.6).

The popular psychologist Oliver James (2007, 2008) refers to this excessive individualism among adults as 'affluenza', which he equates to a disease characterised by an obsessive, but hopeless pursuit of fulfilment through rampant materialism and the urge to economic consumption and display. He argues that 'affluenza' distorts values to the extent that human qualities such as empathy, kindness and love for others become sidelined. In their place is an unhealthy concern with the superficial and the ephemeral. He argues that there is a direct relationship between this distortion of basic human needs and the rising tide of mental health problems throughout the developed world. James, Layard and Dunn agree that children and young people are prey to the forces of rampant consumerism. In particular they are victims of the insidious features of a culture that works by undermining the individual's self-confidence and encouraging a sense of competition and 'one-upmanship' between people. In practical terms this can lead to peer-group problems and bullying, as well as anxiety and depression (Layard and Dunn 2009).

Ironically, some of the problems that children and young persons face appear, superficially at least, to reflect the greater freedoms that they enjoy today compared with earlier generations. As cultures become economically richer, people experience increased freedom from reliance on the collective for financial support, enjoying greater privacy in their living circumstances. This extends to children, who, in rich countries, are more likely to occupy individual bedrooms, and have their own entertainment and communication facilities, such as TVs, computers and mobile phones (Layard and Dunn 2009). These material developments also relate to symbolic factors. Children may not only occupy different physical spaces from their parents, but they also occupy a distinctive and separate subculture. This is dominated by the peer group and what was once referred to as 'youth culture', though in the modern world the non-adult cultural world has many subdivisions within it and is entered well before the dawning of the teenage years.

Layard and Dunn (2009) refer to evidence showing the widening gap between adults and children in terms of the amount of time that children spend with adults as opposed to with their peers. They show how by the age of 11 or 12, children are spending, on average, approximately 5 per cent of their leisure time in adult company and over 50 per cent of this time with peers. As a result, parents and carers are likely to have far less influence on the lives of children than was the case in earlier generations. Whilst there are positive aspects to this, such as rendering children less available to negative influence of adults (e.g. abuse), it may also mean that children and young people have less access to sources of advice and guidance based on experience (Rutter and Smith 1995).

The relative isolation of children and young people from adults has been a source of concern for some time. Rutter and Smith (1995) highlight this phenomenon as a possible cause of the increased incidence of a range of psycho-social disorders in young people since the Second World War, such as delinquency, acting-out and acting-in disorders. The levels of increase seem to be most marked in the more individualistic societies of the world. In an investigation of adolescents' stress management and coping strategies, Gibson-Cline (1996) drew on data from a multi-national study that surveyed the views of over 5000 young people drawn from 13 countries in North America, South America, northern, eastern and southern Europe, Asia, the Middle East and Australasia. Chief among the concerns expressed by young people were worries about their progress in school as well as social and interpersonal difficulties. These concerns were only outweighed by economic concerns in the responses from adolescents living in deprived circumstances. Most striking, however, was the universal finding that 'family institutions [were] ... in crisis and increasingly ill equipped to provide children [with] needed support' (Gibson-Cline 1996, p.268). As a result, adolescents in this study were thrown back to their own limited resources, tending to keep their worries to themselves, or turning to their equally ill-equipped peers for support. The image presented in this study is that of widespread social and emotional upset among adolescents coupled with a lack of personal and social resources for tackling the problems they were facing. Alongside this image of the teenager adrift in a sea of anxiety, is that of the parent, portrayed by Layard and Dunn (2009) and James (2007, 2008), as being far too preoccupied with their own perceived needs and desires.

VOICES FROM POPULAR CULTURE

If readers are sceptical about the argument that there is problem with the way in which children are viewed in certain cultures, then they would do well to read a recent issue of *Observer: Woman* magazine. It contains articles critical of motherhood written by Cooke (2009) and Vernon (2009), followed by a piece entitled: 'Twenty other reasons not to have a baby' (2009). Both authors complain about the 'smugness' of mothers who are preoccupied with their children, and state their own reasons for not wanting to be mothers themselves:

> ...my refusal to have children is...connected to the sense of horror and fear I feel when I encounter a certain kind of mother. What kind of mother is this? She is the kind of mother I talked to at a party the other night, who told me – with no word of prompting from me – about her antenatal classes, in detail, for approximately eight minutes. (Cooke 2009, pp.21–22)

> I really don't like what parenthood does to grown-ups... That pampering cult of Bugaboo-wielding. Mumsnet bothering dullness. (Vernon 2009, p.23)

Both writers indicate that they consider their own lifestyles to be superior to those of the mothers they encounter because of the opportunities created by their child-free state to invest in their careers and leisure pursuits. Vernon in particular seems to sum up the vacuity of a lifestyle infected with what James's calls 'affluenza':

> I like my lifestyle, my career, my body, my capacity to run off to New York at short notice if the opportunity arises. I like that my money is my own to squander. I like that my weekends can be slept away, or read away; that I am not sleep deprived... I like how last minute my life is, how disorganised, how guilt free. I really, really like how certain I am about this. (Vernon 2009, p.23)

A sample from the 'Twenty other reasons not to have a baby' include the following:

- Childless couples dine out twice as often as those with children.

- Working mothers spend more time servicing their personal needs than non-working mothers.

- The frequency with which couples have sex reduces dramatically in the year following the birth of a baby.

- It costs, on average, £140,00, to raise a child and adults with children are more likely to go bankrupt than childless adults.

- Adults without children are able to save a lot of money by taking holidays outside of school vacations.

- Childless women earn, on average almost twice as much as men, whilst women with children earn three quarters of the average male salary.

The apparent message from these three sources is that having children places limitations on the freedom of parents to dispose of their time and income as they might choose. Having babies interferes with adults' pursuit of pleasures of one kind or another. Those adults who take pleasure from having babies, on the other hand, are labelled as 'boring' and leading a 'boring life'. Cooke (2009, p.22) reinforces this line of thinking when she refers to certain children she 'especially like[s]', because they are 'particularly funny and clever', suggesting that children are valued by the extent to which they are entertaining. This resonates with the kind of comments one might expect to see quoted on the billboard outside a theatre or on the cover of a comic novel. It is disturbing that such journalism, whilst employing irony as a rhetorical device, argues that the pursuit of individualism – and, therefore, self-actualisation – is both in competition with and superior to parenting or, as the journalists portray it, motherhood.

The reader may wonder why so much space in the closing chapter of a book rooted in academic scholarship is being devoted to journalistic trivia. We believe that this kind of 'life-style journalism' plays a key role in the process of cultural reproduction. The writers above appear to promote the idea that women who do not bear children are somehow stigmatised by their child-bearing peers, and that there is a new generation of dedicated mothers producing a cohort of 'spoilt', over-indulged children. Whilst it may be argued that there has always been, and probably always will be, a tendency among a proportion of parents to stifle, hot-house and 'spoil' their children, this is, in itself, a reflection of the very self-oriented culture that underlines the kind of journalism discussed here. The evidence we have reviewed in this chapter would suggest an increasing cause for concern in view of the growing number of parents and carers who are insufficiently interested in or engaged with their children as the latter are preventing the former from reaching their goals and leading a fulfilling life.

CONCLUSION: WHY WE NEED CHILDREN

The challenge for the adult in today's society following from the foregoing analysis, is to promote ideas that for some may be challenging and even counterintuitive. We would argue that these ideas are central to the highest aspirations of humankind. After all, it is self-evident that the children of the human race are the future of the human race.

Clearly there is a need to review our cultural values, and the first step would be an acknowledgement of the need for socio-cultural change. The fallacious and misleading nature of what may pass for self-actualisation through materialism and selfishness is one of major targets for intervention. There is no better source to draw on here than the words of Abraham Maslow, who is most closely associated with the concept of self-actualisation:

> Self actualizing people are, without one single exception, involved in a cause outside their own skin, in something outside themselves. They are devoted, working at something, something that is very precious to them – some calling or vocation in the old sense, the priestly sense. They are working at something which fate has called them to somehow, and which they work at and love, so that the work–joy dichotomy in them disappears. (Maslow 1971, p.42)

Self-actualisation as defined above is the antithesis of 'affluenza'. It is concerned with finding deep personal satisfaction in doing good in and to the world. It transcends fashion and petty competition in pursuit of more profound, enduring and intrinsic values. Maslow argues that the pursuit of these values, which include 'truth and beauty and goodness of the ancients and perfection, simplicity [and] comprehensiveness' (p.42), exist as higher level human needs ('meta needs') that when absent lead to what he calls pathologies (or 'sickness of soul'), 'which come from, for example, living among liars all the time and not trusting anyone' (Maslow 1971, p.43).

This resonates strongly with Layard and Dunn's (2009) citation of evidence showing the marked decline in the extent to which people in countries such as Britain believe that their fellow citizens can be trusted, decreasing from 56 per cent in 1959 to 29 per cent in 1999. Not only is the current trend for selfish individualism a distortion of what it means to self-actualise, it also produces social pathologies that prevent individuals from achieving genuine self-actualisation.

Far from being an obstacle to adult self-actualisation, children may thus well be one of the most (if not the most) direct routes to adult self-actualisation. Whether we are the parents of children or child-free adults, we all influence the social and material world in which children are born and grow up. The ways in which children think, feel and behave towards us and each other reflect the values and attitudes of the adult world in which children develop. If as adults we wish to be genuine self-actualisers then we need work towards the creation of a world in which our children develop as well-balanced, emotionally secure and socially engaged citizens. This requires the wider adult world to become more constructively engaged with children and their needs. All adults thus need to become more committed to making our communities safer and more socially cohesive. Parents, communities and schools need to pay more attention to the promotion of the emotional and social wellbeing of children than to the control of children's behaviour. In seeking to achieve these goals, the adult world would need to make itself more open and available to children and their voices. The more adults open up the channels of communication with children and young people, and listen to their perspectives and opinions, the more opportunity there will be for dialogue. Out of dialogue will come the sharing of perspectives and the possibility of a better present and future world for all society, both adults and children.

REFERENCES

Aries, P. (1976) *Centuries of Childhood*. Harmondsworth: Penguin.

Bridgeland, M. (1971) *Pioneer Work with Maladjusted Children*. London: Staples.

Cooke, R. (2009) 'The dummy mummy – boring, selfish, smug: How agnation of women became obsessed with motherhood.' *Observer: Woman*, 38, pp.20–23.

Cunningham, H. (2006) *The Invention of Childhood*. London: BBC Books.

Embry, D. and Biglan, A. (2008) 'Evidence-based kernels: Fundamental units of behavioral influence.' *Clinical Child and Family Psychology Review 11*, 75–113.

Gibson-Cline, J. (1996) *Adolescence: From Crisis to Coping*. Oxford: Butterworth-Heinnemann.

James, O. (2007) *Affluenza*. London: Vermilion.

James, O. (2008) *The Selfish Capitalist*. London: Vermilion.

Layard, R. and Dunn, J. (2009) *A Good Childhood*. London: Penguin.

Maslow, A. (1971) *The Further Reaches of Human Nature*. London: Penguin.

Neill, A. (1968) *Summerhill*. Harmondsworth: Penguin.

Olsen, J. and Cooper, P. (2001) *Dealing with Disruptive Students in the Classroom*. London: Kogan Page/TES.

Patterson, G., Reid, J. and Dishion, T. (1992) *Anti-Social Boys: Vol 4*. Eugene, OR: Castalia.

Pringle, M. (1975) *The Needs of Children*. London: Hutchinson.

Rutter, M. and Smith, D. (1995) *Psychosocial Disorders in Young People*. Chichester: Wiley.

Schoenfeld, N. and Janney, D. (2008) 'Identification and treatment of anxiety in students with emotional or behavioral disorders: A review of the literature.' *Education and Treatment of Children 31*, 4, 583–610.

'Twenty other reasons not to have a baby' (2009) *Observer: Woman*, 38, p.25.

Vernon, P. (2009) 'Why I don't want children.' *Observer: Woman*, 38, pp.23–25.

Wills, D. (1963) *Throw Away Thy Rod*. London: Gollancz.

The Contributors

Claire Beaumont, PhD, is a psychologist and professor at the University of Laval in Québec, Canada. Claire is a researcher at the Centre of Research on Academic Achievement, Co-director of the Canadian Observatory on School Violence Prevention, and President of the Quebec Council for Children with Behavioral Disorders. Claire has been working as a researcher and practitioner in this area for the past 25 years, her main focus or work being students with behaviour disorders and school violence.

Marion Bennathan was Principal Educational Psychologist and Chair of the Child Guidance Service in Avon, UK. She was a founder and first Director of Young Minds, the National Association for Child and Family Mental Health; and editor of its Newsletter. For 13 years, she was also Chair of the Association of Workers for Children with Emotional and Behavioural Difficulties (now SEBDA) and editor of its Newsletter from 1995 to 2002. She represented the Association on government working parties on pupils with SEBD. She was Director of the Nurture Group Network, (now Life President) and author (with Marjorie Boxall) of *Effective Intervention in Primary Schools: Nurture Groups* and of *The Boxall Profile: Handbook for Teachers.*

Mark G. Borg, PhD, is Professor of Educational Psychology at the University of Malta. He has served as Head of the Department of Psychology and Dean of the Faculty of Education. A teacher and a psychologist by profession, he has been engaged in teacher education and researching educational psychology at the University of Malta for 25 years. Professor Borg has served on several national committees including Inclusive Education, School Bullying, and the National Curriculum Council. His pioneering local research in the area of educational psychology has been published, and is acknowledged, widely. Research topics include teacher stress, age position and gender differences in scholastic attainment, teachers' perception of classroom problem behaviour, and school bullying. He has also edited and co-edited the proceedings of two international conferences held in Malta and served on the scientific committee of several national and international conferences.

Carmel Cefai, PhD, is Director of the European Centre for Educational Resilience and Socio-Emotional Health, and a lecturer in psychology at the University of Malta.

He is a visiting fellow at the School of Education, University of Leicester, UK. He is the director of the Masters programme in social, emotional and behaviour difficulties at the University of Malta. He studied education and psychology at the University of Malta and various universities in the UK, completing his PhD in educational resilience at the University of London. His most recent publications include *Promoting Resilience in the Classroom: A Guide to Developing Pupils' Emotional and Cognitive Skills* and *Engagement Time: A National Study of Students with Social, Emotional, and Behaviour Difficulties in Maltese Schools* (co-authored with Paul Cooper and Liberato Camilleri). Carmel is also co-chair of the European Network for Social and Emotional Competence, and co-editor of a new journal *Emotional Education*.

Paul Cooper, PhD, CPsychol, is Professor of Education in the School of Education, University of Leicester. Before taking up his current post, he held academic posts at Birmingham, Oxford and Cambridge Universities. His research interests include social, emotional and behavioural difficulties in schools and effective teaching and learning. He has carried a number of funded research projects in these areas and published more than 20 books and over 100 articles and chapters in edited collections. Between 1994 and 2008 he was editor of the journal *Emotional and Behavioural Difficulties* and he is co-editor of the new journal *Emotional Education*. He is also joint chair of the European Network for Social and Emotional Competence and representative of ENSEC at the European Centre for Educational Resilience and Socio-Emotional Health at the University of Malta.

Caroline Couture, PhD, is Professor at the Department of Educational Psychology at the Université du Québec à Trois-Rivières, Québec, Canada. She is a member of the Centre de recherche et d'intervention sur la réussite scolaire (CRIRES) and of the Groupe de recherche sur les inadaptations sociales à l'enfance (GRISE). She is interested in school provisions and programmes for students with social, emotional and behaviour difficulties. Caroline completed her first degree in educational psychology at the University of Montreal, and her master and doctoral studies at the University of Laval, in Quebec, Canada.

Helen Cowie, PhD, is Research Professor and Director of the UK Observatory for the Promotion of Non-Violence at the University of Surrey. She has established a network of research contacts through her leadership in a series of EU-funded projects, the most recent of which include the Violence in Schools Training Action (VISTA) project, and its development into e-learning format through the Violence in Schools Online Training (VISTOP) project, and a new Cyberbullying Project, each designed to evaluate and disseminate effective anti-violence strategies. She is internationally recognised for her research into peer support as a method for engaging young people themselves in addressing interpersonal difficulties. She has co-authored various books and texts, including *Understanding Children's Development, Peer Support in Action, Emotional Health and Well-being: A Practical Guide for Schools, Managing Violence in Schools* and *New Perspectives on Bullying*.

Knut Gundersen, PhD, is Associate Professor and Director of the Aggression Replacement Training (ART) Centre at Diakonhjemmet University College Rogaland in Norway. He has written several books and articles in the area of social competence, environmental therapy and networking. He has presented at several international conferences around the world, particularly in social competence and ART, coordinates a university course in ART, and has been responsible for introducing, implementing, and evaluating ART in Norway, Iceland and Russia. He is a member of the ICART Board.

Anastasia Karagiannakis, PhD, is a Senior Research Associate for the Canadian Early Intervention Project in the Faculty of Education at McGill University, Canada. In addition, she works as a Psycho-Educational Consultant at the Learning Associates of Montreal, a non-profit community organisation that offers educational services to children, adolescents and adults with learning difficulties. Her research interests focus on behaviour and academic difficulties, peer tutoring interventions, and self-perceptions. She is one of the first Canadian researchers to examine the effects of classwide peer tutoring on the functioning of Canadian children. She has held several travel grants to disseminate research findings at major national and international educational and psychological conferences, published several papers, and supervised students doing research developed from her own work.

Jenny Mosley, founder of Quality Circle Time, and the Director of Quality Circle Time Consultancy in the UK is well known for her inspiring talks, lectures and workshops. Her books and resources have received wide and enthusiastic acclaim. She leads a successful consultancy company that provides unique training for all educators. Her pioneering work was featured in 1991 on *Just One Chance*, BBC, and has received enormous interest from schools and parents. Jenny taught on the MEd programme at Bristol University for 15 years. She wrote the circle time guidance for the UK's DCFS Primary and Secondary National Strategy Social and Emotional Aspects of Learning toolkits (SEAL), and with her commitment to purposeful play she is a member of the QCA Physical Education and School Sports (PESS) Steering Committee.

Ingrid Sladeczek, PhD, is an Associate Professor at the Department of Educational and Counselling Psychology, McGill University, Canada. She is the primary investigator of a national project investigating early intervention policy, practice and services for families and children with developmental delay. Ingrid is one of the few researchers in Canada to investigate the efficacy of problem-solving consultation with parents and teachers of children with behaviour problems and those with developmental delay. She has received funding from various national organisations and foundations, and has published numerous journal articles in this area.

Damian Spiteri, PhD, is Senior Lecturer in Care Studies at the Malta College of Arts, Science and Technology. He worked as a teacher within the substance abuse unit of the Education Directorates, as a social worker with a church-run non-governmental organisation, and as a part-time lecturer at the University of Malta. For a number of years he worked as an educational social worker and as a teacher for a special school with students with social, emotional and behaviour difficulties. His main research interests include the perspectives of young people at risk and psychosocial interventions for this group of young people.

Frode Svartdal, PhD, is Professor of Psychology at the University of Tromso, and teaches also at Diakonhjemmet University College Rogaland, Norway. His main research interests relate to the psychology of learning (operant conditioning, verbal control, extinction), cognitive psychology, and research methodology. He is the author of numerous research articles and books. With Knut Gundersen he has conducted several evaluations of aggression replacement therapy in Norway.

Frances Toynbee, PhD, is Head of Learning Support at Huntington School, York. She set up and was the head teacher of the Pupil Referral Unit in Scarborough, and also alternative provision in Southwark and Lambeth in south east London. She is also regional tutor for the SEBD postgraduate course at Birmingham University. Frances has just completed her PhD at the University of Birmingham on the perspectives of young people with social, emotional and behavioural difficulties on their educational provision. Her main research interests include educational provision for students with SEBD and the perspectives of students with SEBD.

Andrew Triganza Scott was a personal and social education teacher in secondary schools for eight years and President of the PSD Teachers Association. He was also a part-time visiting lecturer in education and psychology at the Faculty of Education and the Faculty of Economics, Management and Accountancy, University of Malta. Andrew is a co-author of *Educational Leaders in the Making*, a book on exploring the developmental and leadership pathways of educational leaders, with Vincent Cassar and Christopher Bezzina. He has carried out various studies and international research collaborations in organisational psychology, social psychology, educational psychology and economic psychology, both locally at the University of Malta and with foreign institutions in Japan, Austria and USA.

Subject Index

Index